Preaching With
Spiritual Passion

THE PASTOR'S SOUL SERIES
DAVID L. GOETZ • GENERAL EDITOR

The Power of Loving Your Church
David Hansen

Pastoral Grit
Craig Brian Larson

Preaching With Spiritual Passion
Ed Rowell

Listening to the Voice of God
Roger Barrier

Leading With Integrity
Fred Smith

LIBRARY OF LEADERSHIP DEVELOPMENT
MARSHALL SHELLEY • GENERAL EDITOR

Leading Your Church Through Conflict and Reconciliation
Renewing Your Church Through Vision and Planning
Building Your Church Through Counsel and Care
Growing Your Church Through Training and Motivation

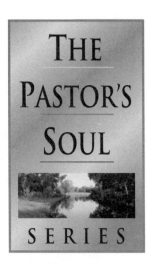

THE
PASTOR'S
SOUL

SERIES

Preaching With Spiritual Passion

ED·ROWELL

David L. Goetz · General Editor

BETHANY HOUSE PUBLISHERS
MINNEAPOLIS, MINNESOTA 55438

Published by Bethany House Publishers
A Ministry of Bethany Fellowship International
11300 Hampshire Avenue South
Minneapolis, Minnesota 55438

Printed in the United States of America by
Bethany Press International, Minneapolis, Minnesota 55438

Library of Congress Cataloging-in-Publication Data

CIP data applied for

ISBN 1–55661–970–7   CIP

To my raving fan
and most honest critic:

my wife, Susan

CONTENTS

INTRODUCTION

AS AN EDITOR OF RESOURCES for pastors, I see just about every new book on preaching that comes off the presses. I'm fortunate to be involved in the field of homiletics at a time when many colleagues are developing a treasury of fresh and practical resources. I've benefited greatly from these and don't know that, if asked, I could contribute anything new to the growing body of knowledge about the craft of preaching.

But for some years now, I have been looking for help with the heart-and-soul issues of preaching. For me, the weekly challenges of sermon preparation and delivery have often been painful, the primary arena in which God has broken me, melted me, and remolded me. I've not always cooperated with God's reshaping of my life and have longed for the benefit of a spiritual guide to help me sort out what was happening in and through me as a preacher. Other than a few lines in Spurgeon's *Lectures to My Students* and Baxter's *The Reformed Pastor*, I haven't found much.

So allow me to get the conversation started.

Preaching like you mean it

Let me state my bias right up front: Preaching matters. Preaching changes lives. Preaching is a big deal. I believe God has gifted, called, even compelled certain of his children to be his mouthpieces, to rightly divide the Word of truth, to love those to whom they preach, to proclaim the Good News like it really is good news, to stand with confidence and boldly say, "Thus saith the Lord."

What proclaimer of God's Word wouldn't want to be described as "preaching with spiritual passion"? No preacher wants to be described, like my mother once described a preacher, "He just doesn't preach like he means it."

"Preaching with spiritual passion" also brings to mind a caricature that repels us. Easily mimicked outward expressions, a strident pitch, an animated tone, volume turned up high—these evoke equal portions of both cynicism and sarcasm. When I was growing up in New Mexico, itinerant evangelists from west Texas often rolled into town with the tumbleweeds. Outfitted with sweat-stained, rumpled suits, shiny cowboy boots, and King James Bibles the size of suitcases, they would shout, stomp, and spit their way through two-week-long revivals like Elijah on steroids. A juvenile mockingbird, I could imitate their cadence and vocabulary with dead-on accuracy, motivated by the laughter of my buddies.

Flipping through the cable channels this past

Sunday morning, I saw their progeny. The new generation is a little more polished, preferring Armani suits, Powerpoint presentations, and studio-styled hairdos, but when I closed my eyes, I heard Brother Bob, my favorite target of mockery, preaching hell hot and heaven sweet.

It has been a while since I caved in to my carnal nature and mocked a preacher. Mainly because now I am one.

I'm sure more than one smarty-pants kid has imitated me behind my back, so I'm a little less judgmental than I used to be. If asked to tell you which preachers are fueled by spiritual passion and which merely have a flair for the dramatic, I wouldn't even hazard a guess. That's because I don't know how they feel about their people. I don't know about their calling. I can't tell if they trust God's Word or their persuasive skills. And I don't know about their faith in the foolishness of preaching.

But when it comes to discerning my own level of spiritual passion, I can tell. I may not want to talk of it with anyone else, but I know whether I'm lifted by hope or drowning in doubt.

Shooting the rapids

Bad Dog. Hell Hole. Twisted Sister.

River guides are nothing if not descriptive. Anyone signing up for a white-water river trip will soon discover the rapids ahead have been given creative monikers, sometimes attributed to the first person who negotiated it, but most often an attempt at creating a word picture of the ride to come. (Tip: My friends Don and Dana recently spent a week rafting the Grand Canyon. They tell me that any rapid with "Falls" in the name is a real bad sign.)

When a guide names a rapid, it doesn't necessarily make it less treacherous or any easier to navigate. Naming it does, however, make it a reality and forces the traveler to prepare for the white water ahead.

My goal in writing this book is to name a few of the bad spots on the river toward spiritually passionate preaching. Critics will rightly discern that this work is descriptive rather than prescriptive. Perhaps others will use my guide to the river as a motivation for drawing better maps, building better boats, or providing more comprehensive training for boat captains.

I'm betting that you, the reader, already have the skills and tools to negotiate this river successfully, but you need a clear idea of what's ahead.

So put on your life jacket and let's push off.

1

THE BRUTAL BULL NAMED "SERMON"

IN THAT TWILIGHT SEASON between pimples and common sense, I began a quest for courage.

In the ranch country of western New Mexico, rodeo was more popular than football or baseball. During the summer months, this sport born of the boredom and recklessness of wild, young cowboys supplied us with recreation, socialization, and competition. There was something for everyone. The girls competed in barrel racing and pole-bending, the boys roped calves and rode broncs and bulls. In the hierarchy of rodeo, bull riding was the sport that separated the boys from the men—at least, that was the way we saw it then. I longed to find out if I was yet a man.

My heroes really have always been cowboys. Larry Mahan, Freckles Brown, and Jim Shoulders inspired courage and perseverance in me and my peers. I determined to follow in the boot prints of these legends of the professional rodeo circuit.

I was fifteen years old in the summer of 1974. I was a little old to begin riding bulls, but it had taken years of relentless pestering to secure my mother's signature on the release form for the Catron County Rodeo. I'd practiced for months on anything I could climb onto—big calves, bony-backed brood mares, our steer being fattened for slaughter, our milk cow, and a bucking barrel: a battered fifty-five-gallon drum hung between four massive poles with car springs and steel cable.

Most of my bull-riding friends had started at the junior level, riding big steers. At fifteen, I was in the senior division. Our opponents would be real bulls, maybe not the fire-breathing demons the professionals rode, but big and bad enough to stomp a shy, skinny kid into apple butter.

On rodeo day I awakened hours before dawn. A dread seized me within moments of awakening. I raced to the bathroom to throw up. After doing my chores and making a failed attempt at breakfast, I loaded my gear into a battered, white-and-red 1961 Ford pickup and drove to the arena. Hours passed before the rodeo started, and bull riding was the final event. The New Mexico sun was not yet heavy, but my shirt was damp with a sweat made rank from terror.

The stock contractor providing the four-legged athletes had pulled in sometime late in the night. The pens were full of roping cattle, bucking horses—and bulls. They rested, and the drone of flies or an occasional horn bumping the pipe rails of the corral were the only sounds. I climbed the fence, wondering which bull would be my dance partner later that afternoon. My throat was pinched dry.

The time passed slowly. I watched my friends who competed in other events, but I didn't really see them. During the girls' barrel racing, I went to find the Porta-johns. Bull riding would be next. I found a vacancy, closed the door, and leaned against it as I fought nausea, confessed all known sin, prepared myself to enter the kingdom, and wept in fear.

Would I die today? Worse, *Would I be revealed as a coward?* I opened my eyes to find a black widow spider dangling just inches from my face. *A bad sign*, I thought. I swatted it with my hat.

That first ride was over in an instant, memorable only for the blinding speed with which I bounced from the ground and climbed the fence. But even in that instant something amazing happened. The fear and apprehension had melted. A heightened sense of clarity and a surreal sense of invincibility welled within me as I strutted back behind the chutes to take off my chaps and spurs. I may not have made it to the whistle, but I had been valiant in the attempt.

As I walked behind the chutes, just moments after facing the greatest fear of my life, a poster tacked to a post announced another youth rodeo the next weekend in Silver City. I would be there. I was a bull rider.

A transaction took place that day. In exchange for my weakness, I found strength. By cashing in my fears, I found freedom. My identity and destiny began to take shape. I was no longer just another nondescript kid at Reserve High School. I had paid my dues, endured the initiation rites, and waged war in the arena. Everyone who knew me knew: *He rides bulls.*

Liars and dreamers

Friends who grew up in suburbia listen to my cowboy stories with a mixture of incredulity and pity. Why would anyone attempt such an insane sport? Any explanation sounds weak. It's about exploring your limits. It's about overcoming weakness. And it's a lot about turning fantasy into reality.

Bull riding occupies much more of one's life than the actual eight-second ride. For days, even weeks before a competition, I would choke back my fears. A dozen times a day I would visualize the sequence of events that I wanted to take place at the next rodeo.

I would straddle the bull in the chute, stroke the tail of that flat-plaited rope until the resin smoked, then slide my gloved hand into the braided handhold as someone pulled the rope tight. I'd wrap the sticky tail around my fist (split-finger wrap with a twist), find my seat, set my spurs, and nod for the gate.

In my dreams, what happened next was a synchronous ballet of power between man and beast. The bull led; I responded with catlike grace. When the buzzer sounded, I would pull the tail of the rope to free my hand, then swing my leg over the bull's hump, landing on my feet with nonchalance. The judges score always put me in first place, beyond the reach of any competitor yet to ride.

The dream did not stop with a trophy buckle and prize money. After the rodeo came the rodeo dance. Surely every buckle bunny in the stands that day had noticed my performance. That night they would queue up for the chance to two-step in my arms, while Johnny Hatch and the Ramblers played "Silver Wings" by Merle Haggard.

These were good—the pre-ride dreams. Their power came from knowing that this was all within the realm of possibility. *This could really happen*, I told myself over and over again.

Better were the post-ride dreams. Like warriors home from battle, young cowboys relived those rides over and over again. Behind the chutes at another rodeo, at school or work, the ritual continued as we provided color commentary for each seconds-long ride in minutes-long detail. We put backspin on our tales, minimizing our brothers' errors of judgment and balance, embellishing the near-death exposure to horns and hooves, all the while illustrating with a pantomime of lifting and reaching, spurred boots hooking the air, free arm reaching for balance.

"I thought you had him covered till your feet got behind you and you slid into the well. If you'da just pushed when he faded, you coulda recovered. Too bad. I reckon you'da been 80 or higher." (Translated, "You never had a chance.")

As we bonded, tales of war eventually led into tales of love. A brief dance with a gum-popping freshman was sculpted into a passionate affair of the heart.

Liars and dreamers then, we were innocent of both death and love.

Not surprisingly, my memories are much fresher than the way things really happened. Some twenty years later, I can still believe my worst rides were good; my best approached some sacred transcendent state.

In reality, most rides lasted just a few heartbeats; more often than not, they were accompanied by bruises, blood, and a shirt stained with manure.

The girls? Not until adulthood did I witness the minimalist interchange between shy adolescent males and wary adolescent females, and then I realized how far afield our fantasies had taken us.

The realities and the dreams of bull riding shaped me in ways I know only a little about. The transaction was emotional—the way I spent money, the crease in my hat, the people I called friends. All these decisions were made from my identity as a bull rider.

A physical transaction also occurred when I first straddled 1,500 pounds of enraged beef. An immediate and significant addiction to adrenaline allowed my hypothalamus to hold my body hostage. Former world-champion cowboy and Grammy-Award-winning singer Chris LeDoux sings, "He's addicted to danger, ruled by passion and pride. To pain and fear he's no stranger, all he knows is he's got to ride."[1]

Even so, several close calls, including a head butt from a bull called Spiderman that left me muddled

---

[1]"Hooked on an Eight-Second Ride," *Watcha Gonna Do With a Cowboy?* Liberty Records.

for days, finally convinced me that I'd never achieve enough glory or riches in the sport to justify all the expense and pain. I'd just have to find my adrenal rush elsewhere. But rodeo had been good to me; it had accomplished its purpose. I knew I was no coward.

Addicted to danger

The day I preached my first sermon (which lasted much longer than my first bull ride), I knew I had found a worthy substitute. The physical risks were minimal in comparison, but emotionally the hazards were world-class. Standing in a pulpit caused my hypothalamus to order up that same delicious punch of fear, hope, and fantasy that it had learned to crave years before.

In *The Maverick Mindset,* Doug Hall and David Wecker write, "Courage has a tangible quality. You can't touch it, but you can feel it. It feels like positive acceleration. Courage sends a rush of energy through your body. It makes you wake up in the morning with a feeling of wanting to wrap your hands around the day."[2]

My courage was put to the test weekly. No eight-second-ride, the sermon lasted thirty minutes. I had six days to savor the event, consider the possibilities,

---

[2]Doug Hall and David Wecker, *The Maverick Mindset* (New York: Simon and Schuster, 1997).

and fear the consequences—then a day to relish and rehash the event. No wonder the Sunday sermon quickly became the axis around which life turned. I have lived and died by the weekly sermon. Monday through Saturday, ideas and possibilities, hopes and fears were churning, colliding, escaping:

- Lives could be changed by this message. *What if I choke?*
- Here's the perfect introduction. *Am I being faithful to the text?*
- Grieving people will find comfort. *Do I really understand this myself?*
- Hard hearts will be melted. *What is my thesis?*
- Broken homes will be restored. *Who am I to speak for God?*
- I think I've got it now. *How little I've prayed.*
- Does anyone ever really listen to the sermon? *But how shall they hear without a preacher?*
- I can't do this one more time. *Woe is me if I do not preach the gospel.*

Then it was Sunday—rodeo time. I stepped into the pulpit, began to speak, and in a heartbeat it was over. I picked myself up out of the dust and walked out of the arena, heart thumping.

How I needed to measure the immeasurable!

A few kind comments from a congregant at the door could be interpreted a hundred ways. Later on I'd ask a hopeful question of my wife, Susan, over dinner, "So, how'd you think it went today?" I often needed not a post-ride analysis but simply the acknowledgment that I was *valiant in the effort.*

Then it was Monday again. Perhaps a bit of dreaming with peers at the coffee shop. But it was time to look ahead. There was another bull to ride. Another week of fighting down fears while preparing to assault the gates of hell once more through the spoken Word.

Surprise transformation

In June of 1995 I left the pastorate. I abandoned the rigors of weekly sermon preparation for a ministry comprised primarily of writing about ministry, especially preaching; editing articles, many related to preaching, and interviewing other preachers. I still preach regularly but usually to strangers. Out of this change came a desire to explore the aspects of preaching that no one talks much about.

This book is mostly about the amalgam of sacred and selfish motives that compel people to preach and to be passionate about preaching. It's a book for preachers who discover that sometimes they are more interested in impressing people than illuminating God. Like bull riding, preaching can turn our guts to water and our brains to shaving cream.

We can't understand our fears and failures without pondering the realization of Paul: "God was pleased through the foolishness of what was preached to save those who believe" (1 Cor. 1:21, NIV).

Most who read that verse won't understand it, but preachers do. You and I are insiders to one of God's greatest surprises: God chooses sometimes foolish people and their sometimes foolish words to change lives. To us belongs the unmerited joy of knowing that God has set *us* apart for this privilege of preaching, and, once in a great while, we see the results of faithful preaching. We elbow each other in the ribs, knowing that preachers are in the running with platypuses as candidates for God's grandest joke.

That I've been granted the gift of preaching has been confirmed over and over again, but that has been countered by an abundant measure of conflict and heartache. I've been swollen with pride and anesthetized by depression. When I read books on the inner life, I sometimes fear I haven't reached even the starting line, much less made any progress in the race.

I have been startled to realize that while preaching has been at the heart of my insecurities, it has also been the primary instrument through which God has been most at work in my journey Christward. I never paid much attention to what God was doing in *me* as I preached; I was mostly worried about what God was doing in *them*. I've begged God to be at work in *them*; we both knew how much *they* needed it!

Yet in the midst of my mixed motives, my fears, my hope, and my hurt, a spiritual transaction was taking place. I understood, sort of, that in the sermon my weaknesses were transformed into something that ministered to others. But what a surprise to find out that *within* me weakness was creating strength and courage.

Volumes of speculation have been written about the nature of Paul's thorn in the flesh. A chronic illness? Depression? Bad eyesight? I think the Scriptures are purposefully vague so we might fill in the blank with our own weakness. Why not preaching with all its inefficiencies and foibles? To me, the text sounds just like a preacher in Monday morning prayers:

"Three different times I begged the Lord to take it away. Each time he said, 'My gracious favor is all you need. My power works best in your weakness.'

"So now I am glad to boast about my weaknesses, so that the power of Christ may work through me. Since I know it is all for Christ's good, I am quite content with my weaknesses and with insults, hardships, persecutions and calamities. For when I am weak, then I am strong" (2 Cor. 12:8–10, NLT).

If "my weaknesses ... insults, hardships, persecutions and calamities" isn't a description of preaching, I don't know what is. Yet, like you, I face the difficulties of preaching. Because I've ridden that brutal bull named "Sermon" week after victorious week after crushing week, I am a changed man, a stronger man. Week after week, a transformation is taking place. Weakness gives way to courage.

2

DOES PREACHING REALLY MATTER?

THE SUN WAS JUST ABOUT TO BREAK over the ridge of Turkey Feather Peak as we rode toward the edge of a large meadow ringed with aspens turning orange and gold. As if on cue, we heard the eerie bugle of a bull elk in full rut.

"Get down," I whispered to my companion. "We'll sneak up on him from here."

"What the (expletive deleted) was that noise?" yelled the fat man on the horse behind me.

"Shut up!" I whispered as loud as I dared. "It's what you came here for."

What about Bob?

Over twenty years ago, I was guiding elk hunters for an outfitter in New Mexico's remote Gila Wilderness. At 8,500 feet above sea level, our fingers were numb from the cold, though it was only the first week of October. My dude for this five-day, trophy-bull hunt was Bob, an accountant from Pensacola, Florida.

We had picked up Bob and four other clients in town the day before. During our trip to camp, two hours in the truck and two more on horseback, I discovered that grumbling Bob had never ridden a horse, slept in a tent, or fired the gorgeous Ruger Model 70 rifle he had purchased for the trip. As we talked about his liabilities, Bob repeatedly stated, "But if I can just get one decent shot, I'll be happy."

Though it was almost dark when we got to camp at Turkey Feather Park, we managed to sight Bob's rifle in. After supper, I explained a few rudimentary facts about aiming for a clean kill. He limped off to bed, already saddlesore: "All I'm asking for is a shot. Just one good shot."

I smirked at Alex, my boss. "You're going to have your hands full with that guy."

The next morning, Alex took a father and son from Dallas down toward the East Fork trail; Chuck took two Border Patrol officers from El Paso on a big circle back toward Willow Creek; and I, chicken little in the pecking order, was stuck with Bob.

Well, all he wanted was a shot.

I knew the whereabouts of a nice, five-point bull near the top of the mountain. I'd been planning to save him for myself; my tag was for the following week of elk season. But after less than twenty-four hours with Bob, I was ready to make sacrifices. I'd get him an easy shot and then he could sit in camp the rest of the week and nurse his sore behind.

That's how we ended up on the mountain that morning.

One decent shot

I had already dismounted and tied my horse. Bob was entangled in his reins, lead rope, camera, binoculars, canteen, and thermos—all tied to his saddle horn and rattling together as he tried to get off his horse. He finally swung his right leg over the horse's back, put it on the ground, and fell flat on his back, his left foot still in the stirrup. His mount, old Buford, looked down at him in disgust. Had it been any horse in the string besides this gentle senior citizen, Bob would have been stomped into a mud puddle, and I could have ridden back to camp in peace.

I managed to get his foot loose, certain by now the elk were somewhere in Arizona. Bob ran around behind Buford and jerked his rifle from the scabbard. He then opened a saddlebag and started slinging sandwiches, Twinkies, toilet paper, and a first-aid kit, digging out a box of .270 cartridges from the bottom of the bag. He jammed shells into his bolt-action rifle, shaking and mumbling, "Just a shot. I just want a shot."

I was about ready for a shot of something myself.

Finally, we started creeping up to the meadow. Amazingly, the bull bugled again and was answered by another bugle. It looked like we might have ringside seats for one of nature's grandest battles, two massive bulls battling for the love interest of an ugly and largely disinterested cow elk.

I could see our quarry thrashing some saplings on the other edge of the meadow. I tried to get Bob down on his hands and knees, but he just didn't bend that well. We finally got behind a deadfall fir tree. When I peeked over the log, the adrenaline rush almost took off the top of my head. There, just over one hundred and fifty yards away, stood a massive six-by-six bull. His antler beams must have been as big around as my forearms. When he threw his head back to bugle, his symmetrical tines reached his flanks. This one might make it into the Boone-and-Crockett record book.

I looked at Bob. He was watching another bull edging into the meadow from the south. Smaller, but still a keeper, he was raising his rifle to shoot when I pointed out the big daddy. Bob grinned and shifted around to face the big bull, now standing broadside to us. Bob steadied his rifle across the log, laid the scope's crosshairs on that little swirl of hair just behind the front leg that points the way to a clean heart-and-lung shot, took a deep breath, held it for an eternity—and squeezed the trigger. *Click.*

He'd forgotten to put a bullet in the chamber.

Bob cursed and jacked the bolt of his rifle, putting a cartridge where it should have been in the first place. Both bulls looked our way, threw their heads back, and trotted off into the thick brush that covered the west side of the ridge. We'd seen the last of those two.

I was so enraged I couldn't speak. Keeping my mouth shut was not due to any innate self-discipline; it had mostly to do with the fact that this guy had paid my boss a thousand dollars to be here, and I wanted to keep my job. I knew of a couple of other places where we'd likely see some elk, but I couldn't stomach the thought of a repeat performance. I wasn't going to waste my effort on someone who would blow a gimme shot like that.

We rimmed around the mountain, largely avoiding prime elk habitat for the rest of the day. After ten hours in the saddle, I hoped Bob would be so sore he'd beg out of tomorrow's hunt.

After supper that night, around the campfire, two of the other hunters shared their success stories while I stewed. Everyone else talked about what they had seen and done that day, and Alex finally asked the wrong question, "Bob, how did your day go?"

Bob didn't tell the group what an idiot he was. He just scowled at me and responded, "I'll be happy if I can get just one decent shot."

It's a miracle I'm not serving a life sentence for murder.

Cynics anonymous

Until I got into ministry, I thought hunting guides and dude ranchers were the most cynical people on the planet. My buddy Bob has many friends, and they all want to go on a western adventure. It can be hard for people who have spent their entire lives around horses, mountains, and guns to tolerate the relative incompetence of those who will pay so handsomely for the privilege of being cold, wet, sore, and hungry. The misery of pleasing an aggravating client is eased only by the chance to tell the story to one's peers.

It may not be much different for pastors. We're well educated. We've spent a good part of our adult lives in study. We attend conferences to keep sharp. We can spend hours in prayer and reflection if we so choose. And on a frequent basis, we are asked to be a spiritual guide for people who, without benefit of our background and experience, can blow the simplest spiritual challenges.

So we gather at the Monday lunch meeting of the ministerial association.

Tales of prima donna musicians, rebel teachers, and perennial soreheads are shared before the salad is even served. Black humor comes with dessert, piping hot with no cream or sugar. "Just blowing off steam," we say. "Just laughing to keep from crying."

But there's a deeper cynicism, the suspicion at our soul's core that the sermon we prepared and delivered with such hopeful anticipation went largely unheard. Maybe the big joke of the universe is they've all gone largely unheard.

I was so proud of my first inductive sermon. I built the tension throughout the message, painting the congregation into a spiritual corner from which there appeared to be no escape. Finally, in the nick of time, I brought the Word of God to light in a way that, brilliantly, in my opinion, made the sanctifying work of Christ make perfect sense.

On the way home, my wife, accustomed to and happy with my usual deductive, linear approach, said, "I couldn't follow you very well today. What were your points?" Perhaps her comment was payback for the times she spent a good deal more time than usual on a special meal or on redecorating a room, and I failed to notice. But such comments make us stop and ask, *Does preaching really matter?*

Sometimes the doubt comes and goes like a mountain spring shower; other times cynical moods settle in like a gray, claustrophobic Chicago winter. In spite of the "nice job" and "good message" heard at the door, sometimes you look around and wonder, *Is anyone's life being changed around here? Are we really making progress?*

Even if there is evidence of change, is preaching really a part of his transformation? Or is it mostly because of his twelve-step group? You know good and well that most people would rather lie like a rug than hurt your feelings.

It's not hard to reach a toxic level of cynicism. I can come to believe that I am preaching to fools who just don't get it. Worse, maybe I'm the biggest fool for wasting my life preparing messages that don't make one slight bit of difference in the lives and hearts of people. While I'll never breathe a word of such doubt to a soul, that is my deepest fear, my greatest insecurity.

As I read the first few verses of Ecclesiastes, I realize I'm not the first preacher to fall into cynicism.

"Meaningless!" says the preacher. "It's all meaningless!" Even when I read his conclusion—"Fear God and keep his commandments, for this is the whole duty of man."—I don't get the sense he has purged cynicism from his soul. To me, he sounds like someone who knows the right answer and says it, even though his mood is still foul.

Fools all around

If preaching is pointless, then all preachers are fools, and I am their king. That much from the apostle Paul can be determined:

> The message of the cross is foolishness to those who are perishing, but to us who are being saved it is the power of God. . . . God was pleased through the foolishness of what was preached to save those who believe . . . but we preach Christ crucified: a stumbling block to Jews and foolishness to Gentiles. (1 Cor. 1:18, 21, 23, NIV)

Who can dispute that the people with whom we share the Word can act in ignorant and foolish ways, much like hunter Bob? In 1 Corinthians 2:14, Paul says, "The man without the Spirit does not accept the things that come from the Spirit of God, for they are foolishness to him, and he cannot understand them, because they are spiritually discerned" (NIV).

Why then hike deeper into the wilderness of preaching when you're pretty sure that, given another opportunity, people will repeat their foolish mistakes?

I had been in a sermon series entitled "Moving Toward Maturity" from the book of James for seven weeks. In just 108 verses, James uses the imperative verb form more than fifty times. I believe the sermonic form should take its cue from textual form, so this series had all the subtlety of the proverbial ton of bricks.

A lot was going on in my life during that period of time. My grandfather had just died. I was battling some chronic health problems. Our most godly layleader was dying of brain cancer. A young couple in whom we had invested significant emotional energy had just left the church in anger. The church had recently paid off a major debt, and the almost inevitable loss of steam occurred—growth and giving dropped far more than the normal summer slump.

Then there was the ecclesiastical equivalent of Chinese water torture—the chronic drip of gossip and malfeasance from a handful of members who had crippled the church for decades. I'd been confronting, working with, and praying for the parties involved for some time, but trying to find the headwaters of the latest rumor is a more perilous adventure than Lewis and Clark ever undertook. My expeditions always led back to the same three or four people, but they would neither admit their guilt nor express even the slightest remorse over the hurt they continually caused.

Fatigue, unresolved emotional pain, and an extended season of conflict had ganged up on me, and cynicism had free reign. Preaching had become a bore and an exercise in futility.

The text for that Sunday was James 3:1–12. In my study that week, you could smell the stench of apathy. I could not get into the spirit of study. You've heard of the sinner's prayer? Well, I prayed the cynic's prayer: *Listen, Lord. If persistent, personal confrontation hasn't stopped the flow of gossip around here, do you really think anyone will listen to a sermon? Come on. Everyone will just think I'm talking to someone else anyway. Don't you think I could better spend my time doing other things? Besides, it's Labor Day weekend and everyone will be out of town anyway. . . . Tell me. What's the point?*

My prayer faded away as my thoughts turned to the big team roping event taking place thirty miles away. After years away from the sport of rodeo, I'd been given the opportunity to compete again. Fact and fantasy merged:

I'm a better roper now than I was fifteen years ago. I've got a great horse, talented partners like Joe, Ray, and Terry. I've got a winning streak going in our roping club. Who knows? I might rope well enough to win one of the trophy saddles being given away.

My daydream was interrupted by a phone call, but my priorities had been set. The sermon was to be hacked out, then I would be free to rope all day Saturday, Sunday afternoon, and all day Monday, Labor Day.

The message was entitled "The Biggest Little Troublemaker." The lack of motivation and creativity coerced me, with only the scarcest bit of regret, to fill in the blanks of a simple outline lifted largely intact from a Warren Wiersbe commentary: The tongue has the power to direct, the power to destroy, the power to deceive.

A few personal illustrations about people who had lifted me and people who had crushed me with their tongues. A nice quote from John White's *The Fight*: "We gossip because we fail to love. When we love people, we don't criticize them. If we love them, their failures hurt. We don't advertise the sins of people we love any more than we advertise our own."[1]

Major emphasis on point number two, with cross references to all the verses in Proverbs that lambaste the gossiper. Close with Psalm 19:14: "May the words of my mouth and the meditation of my heart be pleasing in your sight, O Lord, my Rock and my Redeemer." That was it, I was done. Three hours prep time, max.

Sunday came. I preached. After shaking the hands of the sparse crowd, I ran home, changed clothes, hooked up my trailer, loaded my horse, and drove eighty miles an hour to get to the roping on time. Thoughts of the sermon, those who heard it, and any

---

[1]InterVarsity Press, 1976.

consequence it may have had never caught up with me. The carelessness of it all still frightens me.

Today, looking back over the manuscript and listening to the tape, I can say it was a mediocre, lackluster sermon. Not the worst I've ever preached, but certainly nothing to send in to *Preaching Today*.

Monday I went back to the rodeo arena with thoughts only of my partners' catching three consecutive steers by the horns, so I could rope the hind feet of those same three steers as fast as possible. Ray and I were sitting in third place after two head, waiting our turn for steer number three. The two-hundred-plus teams in our division had dwindled; just twenty or so were still in the running.

I was counting cattle in the chute, trying to figure out which steer would be ours, hoping it wasn't the big, blue-brindle steer that dragged his feet so bad. Jim Wilson hollered at me from across the arena, "Hey, preacher! Your wife's looking for you!"

I rode out to look for Susan amid the catcalls of "Oooh! You're in trouble now, preacher!"

I found her car. She was obviously upset. I quickly noted that she and the two kids appeared to be fine. *Dang it. I'm just one steer away from possible fame and fortune. This better be important.*

"What's up?"

"It's Ruby. She had a massive heart attack this morning, and they don't think she's going to make it."

Numbness. Fear. Guilt. More fear. Adrenaline

surge. Ruby was the undisputed queen of gossip in our community. *My God, was it. . . ? No, no way. This had nothing to do with that sermon. Just coincidence. Wasn't it?* I saw in Susan's eyes the same questions.

Someone yelled at me: "Ed! You're up! Get in there before you forfeit!"

I loped back to the arena while building a loop, backed my buckskin into the box, and nodded at my partner. Off we went. A perfect head catch, nice easy turn, smooth rhythm. Perfect. I fired, and missed, sticking my rope in the dirt.

"Sorry, Ray," I muttered, too much in shock to be embarrassed. I loaded up and drove to the hospital.

I wonder how Peter felt after Ananias and Sapphira dropped dead following his confrontation in Acts 5? Verse 11 says, "Great fear seized the whole church and all who heard about these events." In our small town, word spread like head lice about the sermon and its apparent effect. Later that week at the Donut Shack, one of the old, whiskered coffee hounds walked over to my booth and said, "Hey there, Pastor Ed. Whatcha preachin' about this week?" He leaned close and winked at me. "I don't want to be yer next casualty!"

Ordinarily, I would have given it right back to him, but I couldn't laugh. Ruby was still in critical care.

I spent much of my study time that Tuesday on the floor on my face, trembling. For the first time I had a visceral understanding of the biblical phrase "the fear of the Lord." God could have chosen to smite me instead, as a visible demonstration of the dangers of handling holy things with nonchalance. He could have made an example out of me for my lack of faith in his ability to sanctify his children.

When I stood to preach the next Sunday, I was still shaking. I've never encountered such an attentive audience. We continued our way through the third chapter on James, wanting desperately to pretend that last Sunday had not happened the way it did. Yet we had seen the hand of God, and we were sore afraid. That message might not have been a great homiletical masterpiece, but I can tell you this much—both preacher and congregation were fully engaged that Sunday. We had seen something in our midst that convinced us that preaching had power.

Unlike Ananias and Sapphira, Ruby lived to gossip again. Amazingly, she seemed to be the least affected, at least spiritually, by what had happened. But a lot of the rest of us thought twice about passing on a juicy bit of news, even under the guise of a prayer request.

Not everyone, though: After one couple left the church, word on the gossip chain, er, prayer chain was that their leaving was because of "what Pastor Ed did to Ruby."

I wouldn't call what happened next revival, but there were some subtle changes over the following few months. Attendance picked up again. I had numerous conversations about spiritual matters with people who had previously revealed little spiritual bent. Two people with whom I had been sharing Christ came to faith in those weeks. Wednesday night prayer meetings took on a new tone of seriousness about the task of intercession as a few newcomers started attending and a few old-timers quit coming.

Giving increased as well. James 5 was coming up, and perhaps no one wanted to be in my sermonic sights when we got to the subject of stewardship! Following a well-attended world missions conference, our Christmas missions offering was the largest in the history of the church.

We celebrated the season of Advent that year, a radically new idea for our decidedly non-liturgical community of faith. A community Christmas Eve service saw our church packed to the rafters. We finished the year strong. God finally had our attention.

Or should I say, God had *my* attention.

My wife doesn't remember that sermon as a pivotal point in the life of that church. Maybe the only real change in the congregation happened within me. Maybe it was mostly a time of personal revival. Some unconfessed pride and ambition were exposed and rooted out. Ever since, I've preached with more of a passion, with a faith in my task that has seldom wavered.

Witness to power

I used to laugh when Barney Fife told someone that his hands were registered with the FBI as lethal weapons. I really wonder if preachers should register their Bibles, their notepads, their pulpits. Nothing has fueled my passion for preaching more than the profound belief that preaching really matters. God can use the sermon to bring about an incredible transformation in the lives of his people. Now when cynicism begins to seep into my life, I recall when I've seen lives changed, and more importantly, I recall the times God has used the sermon of another to bring about a change in my life.

More than anyone, Paul knew the power of the sermon. In his introduction to the Romans, he wrote, "That is why I am so eager to preach the gospel also to you who are at Rome. I am not ashamed of the gospel, because it is the power of God for the salvation of everyone who believes . . ." (Rom. 1:15–16, NIV).

Amen and amen. Cynicism loses its grip on the preacher who has witnessed the power of God move as a result of the sermon.

Then to the Corinthians: "My message and my preaching were not with wise and persuasive words, but with a demonstration of the Spirit's power, so that your faith might not rest on men's wisdom, but on God's power (1 Cor 2:4–5, NIV).

Not long after these events, I wrote these words in my journal:

Come, Holy Spirit. Demonstrate your power again and again, that my faith might rest in God and not in my puny attempts at wisdom and persuasion. Change lives through my sermon. And begin, right here, with me.

3

PATIENCE FOR SOREHEADS

SOME PEOPLE PAY a bigger price to minister than others. Take my friend Tim, for example:

After Bible college, he went to work for a parachurch ministry. He was completely sold out to the cause; the organization's membership requirements were so stringent, his friends wondered if he had gotten involved in a cult. His job involved doing all the front work for an evangelistic team.

My buddy would arrive on a college campus the day before an event, often bribing the security guy with a box of donuts before he could set up the stage, lights, and sound. The next morning, he would crank up some loud music while a crowd gathered. The main speaker was a name you would recognize, a popular guy who literally wrote the book on apologetic evangelism. Sometimes he would preach, other times he would debate some professor from the philosophy department. Either way, it was always interesting. The organization saw some people get saved, made a whole lot of people mad, even got in a few fights.

In between passing out flyers, going out for coffee and sandwiches, and running the lights and sound,

47

Tim very occasionally got on stage to share his testimony. But then, while the speaking team was on a flight headed home, Tim was left behind to pick up the mess and smooth over relationships with the local ministers.

After a couple of years, Tim had had enough of the itinerant stuff. He longed to settle into a local parish and minister out of the limelight. Tim's mentor dropped his name in the hat of a big suburban church that had gone through a couple of pastors in quick succession. Informed sources described the church to Tim as "having lots of potential."

When the search committee came calling, Tim answered.

He didn't have the boxes in the garage unpacked before the fecal matter hit the rapidly revolving cooling unit. The church's troubles started at the top. A number of the elders and deacons were of questionable moral stature. They were noted in the community for their lack of scruples. Their marriages and families were in shambles, and several had problems with substance abuse. With few exceptions, their wives were vicious gossips.

Tim sized up the situation pretty quickly, and on his third Sunday he blistered them with an angry sermon on character and holy living. They politely ignored him on their way out the door, but to one another they said, "That's one."

Then there was the matter of a couple of popular Sunday school teachers who could really draw a crowd. The only problem was their definition of orthodoxy was broader than the San Fernando Valley. One guy, for example, taught a class on comparative creation myths. He had a Powerpoint presentation with cool graphs and charts that compared and contrasted the Genesis account of the flood with the Sumerian Epic of Gilgamesh. He had one slide of Noah and Utnapishtim squaring off in a wrestling ring, just like Hulk Hogan and the Ultimate Warrior. People loved it, but attenders left class each week believing one was as fake as the other.

Tim had a much higher view of Scripture. He drew a line in the sand, requiring teachers to sign an agreement of basic doctrinal standards.

"That's two," they said in the parking lot after the meeting.

The church constituency was sophisticated, highly educated, and loaded with dough, which, frankly, intimidated Tim. They were giving zip to missions and community outreach, and that, frankly, infuriated Tim. He knew firsthand what it meant to be down and out. He had grown up in a trailer park in the stereotypical small town: Tastee-Freeze at one end and farm-equipment dealer on the other. His dad was a trucker who, not long after Tim's birth, quit coming home. His mom raised him on a waitress's salary, with a little help from Grandma's pension.

Tim couldn't stand the thought of such an affluent church with a core value of miserliness. He took on the budget committee, asking it to ante up 20 percent of the budget for missions and appointing a task force to investigate community needs, especially to single mothers.

"That's three" went the conversation on the prayer chain that week.

In addition, Tim was quite a bit younger than the majority of his congregants, and he was also cursed with a baby face. His mentor had told him once, only partly in jest, that he needed two things to be successful in ministry—gray hair and hemorrhoids. The gray hair, he explained, would make Tim look distinguished, and the hemorrhoids would make him look concerned.

Tim was forced to minister without the benefit of either.

Though the search committee and elder board assured Tim the reason they wanted a younger pastor was to reach young families, they insisted he do it with a worship style that had ceased being culturally relevant just after the war. Tim would not acquiesce; he blew them away one morning with a worship band. To make it worse, the drummer had a ponytail, and was known to work nights in a local bar band.

Just how the upright church members knew this, no one could say, but one thing was sure—*that was four.*

What do you do when you've used up all your downs and you haven't moved the football even a yard?

Tim first got an ulcer, then he e-mailed his mentor—"I'm dying out here. You gotta tell me what to do."

As it happened, the old guy was taking a hiatus from the road and promised to come as soon as he could. In the meantime, he took the time to write from his new residence. Here's the word that came back from AposPaul@jailbird.com:

> Until I come, devote yourself to the public reading of Scripture, to preaching and to teaching. Do not neglect your gift, which was given you through a prophetic message when the body of elders laid their hands on you.
>
> Be diligent in these matters; give yourself wholly to them, so that everyone may see your progress. Watch your life and doctrine closely. Persevere in them, because if you do, you will save both yourself and your hearers. (1 Tim. 4:13–16, NIV)

I *know* Timothy. I *feel* for Timothy. Man, I *am* Timothy. Been there, done that, got the T-shirt, the souvenir cup, the scars, *and* the ulcer. When I read Paul's counsel in 1 and 2 Timothy, I feel like these letters were intended for my mailbox. I've dealt with every issue Timothy faced in Ephesus, and like him, I had to stand in the pulpit every week and face the crowd, sometimes not knowing for sure who was friend and who was foe.

I'm probably most qualified to discuss how *not* to

preach during church conflict. Almost half my years in the pastorate were spent in a congregation whose predisposition to conflict was in its genetic code. Much of what I have to say about preaching with passion in the midst of conflict I learned by doing the wrong things first:

- I've stood up and pretended everything was okay when everyone *knew* it wasn't.
- I've confused the crowd by making thinly veiled references to conflicts only a few knew anything about.
- I've hid behind the pulpit and said things I wasn't brave enough to say in board meetings.
- I've rooted through the Scriptures selecting heart-seeking missile texts to preach with specific targets in mind.
- I've lost my focus on reconciliation and actively pursued retaliation.

I've probably done all of the above on the same Sunday. Time and again God has graciously brought me back to Paul's advice to Timothy. In times of conflict, I'm sorely prone to ignore the gift of preaching and to watch everyone's life and doctrine but my own.

Here are several lessons I've learned in those times of rebuke:

1. *Keep public-relation promotions out of the pulpit.* During one stretch of conflict, while confiding in an old seminary buddy who pastored half a continent away, I described the parties behind the conflict, their

ungodly motives and their Philistine tactics, then moved on to assert my own dovelike innocence and Christlike conduct. My buddy stopped me.

"Now hold on just a minute," he said. "I'm having a hard time believing those people are as evil as you say, and I know you ain't as full of sweetness and light as you just described yourself. Think maybe you're overstating the case a bit?"

Of course not.

But I've noticed *others* tend to sanitize and saintize their motives. If I *were* to magnify the purity of my own actions and motives, I'd pay attention to the kind of personal illustrations I used in preaching. And I'd be sensitive to the temptation to use the pastoral prayer to underscore subtly but surely my spiritual and moral superiority. I knew I had sunk to a new low when I caught myself directing my prayers toward the people listening in and not to the Father.

In conflict, the ever-present temptation to use the pulpit to make ourselves look smarter, funnier, and kinder than we really are increases, but the pulpit is no place to conduct a public-relations campaign.

A few days after the death of Princess Diana, Queen Elizabeth made a short but memorable address to her bereaved nation. While such a speech was unusual, some reporters said the Queen's uncharacteristically personal speech was delivered primarily to counter the perception that the House of Windsor was cold and uncaring. Prince Charles allegedly told his mother if she didn't speak out, that would be a public-relations nightmare for the already beleaguered royal family.

Crocodile tears usually reveal crocodile teeth. Self-promotion is seldom effective.

2. *Get it out of your system before stepping into the pulpit.* Most often, preaching will not be the primary means by which we solve conflict that revolves around personalities; that is a private matter best settled face-to-face. Matthew 18 indicates public discourse is the last resort in a reconciliatory process.

Unless there is a rampant corporate sin that affects a majority of people, my goal during conflict is to preach as I would under normal circumstances. The temptation to vent is just too enticing. Angry preaching is a mutation of passionate preaching, but not the kind of energy I can run on for long. Anger is the high-octane fuel that burns white-hot, but it always causes damage. When angry, I usually deliver the kind of message I long regret.

In a recent LEADERSHIP article, Calvin Miller, former pastor and writer-in-residence at Southwestern Baptist Seminary, recalled the time someone preached a message in seminary chapel entitled "Are There Any Fat Cows of Bashan on Seminary Hill?" It seems that just about everyone on campus showed up to find out if there were any and left convinced that there were, but they personally were not counted among the bovine.

That response is typical. Too often the people I've wanted to blister from the pulpit either don't show up that Sunday or don't seem to recognize when I'm talking directly to them. By venting in the pulpit, I run the risk of alienating those who have yet to jump into the fray.

3. *Spend time with both enemies and friends.* I tend to vacillate between introversion and extroversion. When things are going well, I draw energy from people, but in conflict I can become a recluse. Not wanting to run into the opposition, I'm tempted to stay behind the books. And since I'm not that good at hiding my feelings, I'm equally afraid of running into a friend who might ask, "So, how's it going?"

When I gave in to my inclination to hide, my preaching inevitably suffered. There is information in the opposition. And there is encouragement and support from those who aren't participating in the current round of fighting. In one church, my cross to bear was an electrician named Wally. He was both a church leader of considerable influence and a habitual liar. The first couple of times I realized he wasn't shooting straight with me, I gently confronted him.

His denial was so vehement I backed off—maybe I had been wrong. But then I began to watch how others in the church reacted to him. Suffice it to say: this was a sick family system, and Wally had surrounded himself with enablers who aided and abetted his frequent inexactitudes.

The only way to discover what was reality and what was reality only to Wally was to spend time with him. As I continually made excuses to be with him, I found out he was generous, talented, and actually pretty likable. But he lived at such a high level of overcommitment that he was constantly lying to get himself out of a pickle—at work, at home, at church. I learned how to get information from him without forcing him into a corner where he had to lie to cover his failure. And I always gained some information that I could take with me to the pulpit.

As an influencer, he had the inside scoop on the other long-term families of the church, and I gleaned many insights into the motives and methods of my antagonists. Those insights helped me apply my preaching in ways that dealt with the issues *behind* the conflict.

For example, I found out that one couple who made life particularly hard on me was living with the guilt, anger, and shame of a son who had adopted a promiscuous homosexual lifestyle. That family was on my mind on occasions like Mother's Day and Father's Day. The Sunday I preached about the Prodigal Son, though the text is primarily about Father God as the seeker of lost children, I was able to acknowledge the pain of parenting a child who rejects the values of his or her parents. I live with the hope that the emotional iceberg blocking our relationship melted just a bit on those days.

In that same church was an elderly couple who honestly believed I was the heir to Billy Graham. Every Sunday, I knew just where to look to find their smiling faces and a nod of affirmation as I preached.

During several periods of congregational uproar, I made a pastoral visit to their country home. Though we never discussed the conflict, over pie and coffee they affirmed me, prayed for me, and sent me back into the fray. I would never have found that source of hope and encouragement if I'd stayed sequestered in the study.

4. *God has charged me to love these soreheads.* When hampered by a handful of church soreheads, I'd like to have a comeback like Elijah did in 2 Kings 2. The prophet was being harassed by a crowd of baggy-pantsed kids with odd hair and body piercings. They kept circling Elijah on their skateboards, making fun of his follicularly-challenged condition. The Bible says he turned around, looked at them, and called down a curse on them in the name of the Lord. Then two bears came out of the woods and mauled forty-two of the youths.

What I want to know is, where exactly is that curse found?

I'm not balding, but I think knowing how to call down a curse in the name of the Lord would come in handy in all kinds of situations, especially during periods of church conflict. But since I can't do that, the next best thing would be to preach the text with the *implication* that I know how to call in the bears, so people better not mess with me. I'm just kidding, of course. Mostly. At times I've wondered if that noted theologian Al Capone was right when he said, "You can get a lot farther with a kind word and a gun, than a kind word alone."

A preacher's chief antagonists, however, will not be strangers.

They will be the people to whom God has charged the pastor to love and develop, often people in whom we have invested significant amounts of time and energy. When a fight breaks out, there is no more crucial time to demonstrate publicly the love of a pastor's heart.

In *The Reformed Pastor*, more than 300 years ago, Puritan preacher Richard Baxter said:

> If ministers were content to purchase an interest in the affections of their people at the dearest rates to their own flesh, and would condescend to them, and be familiar, and affectionate, and prudent in their carriage, and abound, according to their ability, in good works, they might do much more with their people than ordinarily they do. . . . Labour, therefore, for some competent interest in the estimation and affection of your people, and then you may the better prevail with them.[1]

Baxter's right, of course. While Al Capone enjoyed a certain amount of success in his chosen profession, he would have made a lousy preacher.

---

[1] Richard Baxter, *The Reformed Pastor* (Carlisle, Pa.: Banner of Truth, reprint 1979). First published in 1656.

4

OVERCOMING THE
WEEKLY WEARINESS

IT WAS THE LAST ELK HUNT of the season. Three of our four clients had been successful early in the week, and we were hunting hard to make sure the other guy didn't get skunked. No luck. On the next-to-last day of the season, the snow came: wet, heavy, and deep. Alex, my boss, made the judgment call: "We've got to get these guys out of here. We'll ride out today, then you and I will come back and take down camp."

We loaded their gear, meat, and antlers on the pack mules and started out. The mules U-shaped feet were better prepared for this winter work than their equine half-brothers. Snow balled up in the horses' rounder hooves until they were walking on stilts of packed ice, making them prone to stumble—not a good thing on the narrow trail that switched back across several deep canyons. It took most of the day to get down the mountain to Willow Creek, where the trucks and horse trailer were parked. From there we had forty miles of dirt road to navigate before we hit the pavement, then another thirty-five miles to our homes in Apache Creek.

Ten animals would never fit in the trailer, so we left the four mules and one horse behind in a nearby Forest Service pasture to be picked up the next day. We drove most of the night in four-wheel-drive low gear, sliding off the road on two different occasions, having to winch ourselves out of the drifts. We said good-bye to our hunters as we dropped them off at the Rode Inn motel, drove home, caught two hours of sleep, ate breakfast, then started back up the mountain. During the night, the snow had stopped, the sky cleared, and the temperature plummeted. The snowplow had been up the mountain past Rainy Mesa to the Gilson ranch but had turned around about ten miles short of where our animals were. We knew we could never drive back into our camp in the Gila Wilderness under those conditions, but somehow, we had to get those animals out.

So we started walking, carrying halters and lead ropes.

Were I to design the ultimate aerobic exercise machine, it would simulate walking in knee-deep, wet snow at high altitude. This was in the days before synthetic fibers, and our clothes were soon soaked with sweat. We trudged on, stopping only to ease our pounding hearts.

When we finally made it to Willow Creek, the mules were their usual stubborn selves, refusing to be caught without playing hard to get. They were not broken to ride, so we took turns riding the lone horse, bareback, while the other man walked—each leading two half-wild mules. The sun was already setting in the pale, winter sky as we started following our tracks back down the old logging road.

The way back was somewhat easier than the way in; we were going mostly downhill, and the person walking had the benefit of the rider and other animals tromping down the snow. But we were wet, cold, and hungry—perfect candidates for hypothermia. We both ended up walking, it was too cold riding. Hours passed. The moonlight reflecting off the snow created a surreal world in which time stood still. I wondered what death would feel like, imagining it to be warm and restful. We staggered on, falling too many times to count.

The sight of that truck and trailer made us nearly weep with relief. After loading the animals, we climbed into the truck cab and cranked up the heater. Uncontrollable shivering helped keep us awake long enough to get home. Alex's wife fixed us pancakes, bacon, and eggs while we cared for our hungry and thirsty pack string. A hot meal, hot shower, and four-teen hours of sleep later—I was good as new, except for the frostbitten ears that plague me even now when winter comes to call.

Spiritual fatigue

Acute fatigue is also a reality of pastoral ministry. The busyness of the Christmas or Easter season can put the hurt on us every year—but it passes. And the all-night youth lock-in (which, I'm convinced, is Satan's tool to drain the small-church pastor) can be brutal—but it's only one night.

Tougher to shake are the nights in the emergency room with a family while a loved one struggles between life and death. Those periods of intense pastoral care can sap every bit of strength we possess, especially since these events invariably happen late in the week when a sermon must be delivered before we can recharge.

I still grow weary remembering the weekend that began with a Friday funeral, followed on Saturday by another funeral *and* a wedding, then of course, Sunday. At least the wedding and the sermon had been anticipated. Such experiences can suck pastors dry, and steps must be taken to rest and lay low for a while. Acute fatigue can pass fairly quickly if proper steps are taken.

Far more treacherous is the chronic state of fatigue that sneaks up on us while we are enjoying ministry. It wraps its cold tentacles around us. The slow squeeze begins, and we find ourselves gasping for breath, wondering why we are losing our passion for preaching.

Passionate preaching is itself physically draining. To invest so much energy and emotion in study, then to funnel that distillation of soul into a single event is to invite an emotional and spiritual crash. Delivering the message two or three times in multiple services simply raises us to a greater height from which to fall later that day.

Common sense tells us to go home immediately after the service and crawl back into bed. If we can manage to work in a nap, experience tells us that someone will call just as we slip into a coma. Our conditioned response, even while still mostly unconscious, is to pick up the ringing object and hold it to our ear, then exhale a hearty "Hello!" in a chirpy tone that says, "Of course I wasn't sleeping!"

The grating voice on the other end of the line informs us that Mrs. Albright won't be returning to our church because she was offended by the behavior of two children seated in front of her, and if that's the kind of chaos that passes for worship, well, she'll just find another place where people understand that worship means silence and reverence, and people have enough Christian values to discipline their children, and why doesn't Ruth Peabody sing anymore? Am I upset that her husband now works for the state lottery, and do I think I'm better than anyone else because I. . . .

Someone's mad. At me. For something. Again. Major or minor, all gripes feel major in the fog of post-sermon fatigue.

Sunday naps for most pastors are in that same fantasy realm as the call from the megachurch search committee and the heartfelt apology from the deacon board. Sunday is the day ripe for connecting with folks who slow down just a little more on this day than any other. More Sundays than not, my wife and I had dinner guests or were dinner guests.

Churches of my faith tradition have long held that attendance at the Sunday night service is the measure of the true believer. (They even expect the preacher to show up!) For the pastor who has just done battle with the principalities of darkness in the heavenly realm, it's hard to do much better than a bad imitation of Sunday morning in the evening service.

When I become the Protestant Pope, I'll declare the Sunday evening service, as it still exists in many churches, *anathema*. But for now, many preachers still have to stumble back to the pulpit, feeling grateful if they've managed to scratch out an outline during the football game. That's a best case scenario. I'm convinced the majority of pulpit plagiarism happens between two and six on Sunday afternoons. We're driven to it by our fatigued state.

Why, then, are we so surprised when Monday dawns and we struggle just to stand upright and not drag our knuckles on the ground? Coffee—strong, black, gallons of it—jacks us into an induced state of semiconsciousness.

Just as we're starting to feel like living another day is an option, the old Steve Miller Band tune runs through our heads: "Time keeps on slippin', slippin', slippin' into the future." We stare at the calendar and begin to blubber uncontrollably, because even in a numbed state, we recognize another Sunday is just 144 hours away—and the clock's ticking. Worse, in many cases, we are expected to bring an inspired word from the Word at the Wednesday evening service, a mere 60 hours from now.

Just as chronic fatigue will kill sexual passion, it can stifle spiritual passion. Worse, fatigue makes maintaining intimacy with God almost impossible. In a desperate state, we start coming to God's Word for sermon fodder, not to fill our souls.

Passion dies. In its place is either a void, or a hastily constructed, unconvincing facsimile of the real thing.

A thousand times while growing up, I heard my parents or grandparents yawn, stretch, and say, "There's no rest for the wicked." To which the conditioned response was always "And the righteous don't need any."

With all due respect to my ancestors, what idiot thought that one up?

Even as a kid I knew that maxim was stupid, but a cursory review of my life's work habits reveals I have come to believe it on some level—either the lack of rest in my life was punishment for my vile ways or the inevitable consequence of doing the Lord's work.

For the past twenty-plus years, I've either had jobs that easily expanded to fill all available hours in the week, or worked two jobs, or had multiple part-time jobs while working on a full-time education.

When I left a full-time pastorate to join the editorial staff at LEADERSHIP, I had daydreams about a Monday-through-Friday, eight-to-five schedule.

Within weeks, I was as busy as ever, working late into the night rehabing an old house, supply-preaching many weekends, hustling free-lance writing projects, and hosting and attending barbecues to get to know our new neighbors.

For years I told myself the reason for my fatigue was the pressures of the pastorate. Now I have to face the fact that the problem is somewhere in me.

I have friends who are professional rodeo cowboys. In their quest to make the National Finals each year, they push themselves to compete in more than a hundred rodeos over ten months, often driving all night to get to the next one. As one said to me a few years ago, "It's not the bulls that will wear you down, it's seeing too many sunrises through the windshield of a pickup." Like other professional athletes, most rodeo cowboys see their careers end sometime around their thirtieth birthday.

Preachers make it a little longer, but the comparison is valid: It's not the sermons that wear you down, it's the failure to allow the body and soul to recover from the trauma of preaching.

Several attitudes prevent us from pausing long enough to refuel:

1. *Too unrealistic.* During the 1997 NBA Championship series between the Chicago Bulls and the Utah Jazz, I watched Michael Jordan play an incredible game while suffering from a gnarly case of either flu or food poisoning. *Yup,* I thought. *That's the way we champions perform, never letting the inevitable ups and*

downs of life keep us from playing at the top of our game.

That thinking is nothing more than another trip to Fantasy Island. I'm not Michael Jordan, and the inevitable ups and downs of life *will* keep me, at times, from playing at the top of my game. As much as I love preaching, during some stretches I was simply unable to preach as well as I would have liked. Following the births of both of our daughters, the priority of preaching went into a freefall for a couple of months while I focused on my family. During a year-and-a-half bout with a baffling illness, getting better was my main concern, not homiletics.

I've had preacher friends who struggled to keep their marriages intact, others who have had to deal for years with a prodigal son or daughter. Is it reasonable to expect anyone to care passionately about a sermon in such difficult circumstances?

Solomon wrote, "There is a time for everything, and a season for every activity under heaven." Authentic, passionate preaching may not always be possible when chronic life issues pin us to the mat.

2. *Too demanding.* They say that self-employed people work for the most demanding bosses. Most preachers face their toughest critics when they look in the mirror. Even more relentless than the ever-approaching Sunday are personal expectations. Those who become chronically weary often swing for the fence every time they preach.

Our best motives are fueled by a genuine passion to see people become passionate about their relationship with God. Unfortunately, our motives are sometimes mixed with grandiosity. This is essentially a theological problem, evidence we aren't clear about the role of the Holy Spirit, whose job is not up for grabs.

We can forget the efficacy of consistent preaching intentionally focused over the long-haul. Effective sermon planning not only relieves the week-to-week panic of what to preach, it allows us to plan to say in many weeks what we cannot hope to say in only one. While one sermon may occasionally be the catalyst for change in someone's life, more often lasting change is the result of a steady diet of biblical challenge and encouragement.

3. *Too driven.* Few books have shed light on the chronic fatigue of ministry like Archibald Hart's *Adrenaline and Stress.*[1] I now understand that adrenaline, that necessary and welcome component of passionate preaching, has an hangover effect that can cripple our effectiveness—something I failed to recognize for years.

For much of 1993 and 1994, I lived with a level of fatigue that depressed me and perplexed my doctor. After much blood work to rule out everything else, I was diagnosed with fibromyalgia, a neuromuscular syndrome that results in chronic muscle and joint pain, sleep disorders, and depression—symptoms I still endure on an off-and-on basis.

But after reading *Adrenaline and Stress,* I've won-

---

[1]Archibald Hart, *Adrenaline and Stress* (Dallas, Tex.: Word Publishing, 1995).

dered more than once if my symptoms were (are) the inevitable result of living too long in an adrenaline-saturated state. If only I had planned for the Monday adrenaline hangovers, if only I had allowed time to dry out between Sunday binges—if only I had taken the Sabbath seriously.

Sabbath yearning

For me to promote the necessity of a consistent Sabbath is like Mick Jagger pounding the pulpit for abstinence from sex, drugs, and rock 'n' roll. Who could listen without laughing? That's why I encourage every pastor to read Eugene Peterson, former pastor and now professor at Regent College in Vancouver, British Columbia.

To paraphrase G. K. Chesterton, it's not that the Sabbath has been tried and found wanting; it is that it has been tried and found difficult. Everyone who fights the passion-draining work of ministry instinctively knows that the Sabbath is the solution. But it seems like a solution beyond our ability to grasp. Compressing the necessary work of a congregation into six days seems an amazing feat, yet research shows many pastors manage to take a day off each week.

How do most of us spend it, though?

Changing the oil in the car, mowing the lawn, reading for a D. Min. course, coaching the youth soccer team, taking down the Christmas lights, giving the dog a lift to the vet to get neutered, and, inevitably, spending just a little time on the next day's sermon. What separates this day from the other six is not the cessation of work but the focus of work. Work is work, not rest. A day away from ministry is necessary, and may even be enjoyable, but it's no Sabbath.

The Sabbath restores energy, hope, and passion. Observing the Sabbath means refraining from the work that saps us of energy, hope, and passion. Sabbath means putting the myth of "busy is better" to death. It means a new way of thinking about time, priorities, and recreation.

My theological default setting is on Legalism. My first thoughts on Sabbath are that it must be *spiritual*, a day spent on my knees in a prayer closet, pouring out my sins, my grief, and my anguish to God. A few years ago, at the point of a critical decision, a friend let me use his mountain cabin, where I spent forty-eight hours in prayer and fasting. I counted those days as my days off for that week. While it was a significant time, I came home exhausted. It took weeks to get back to normal. On reflection, I'd say that time away was a necessary and welcome spiritual exercise but no Sabbath.

In the days prior to the technological age, work for most people meant physical labor. The idea of Sabbath rest for those people meant a cessation from physical labor. The normally taboo options of sedentary activities or even inactivity were lifted for one day a week. The mind was set free from the mundane business of labor to explore theology, music, and conversation.

For pastors, as well as many others whose work is defined by physical inactivity and mental flurry, perhaps the Sabbath should involve sweat and sunshine and the cessation of reading, thinking, counseling, and relating.

During my years in Arizona, I found Sabbath in the most unexpected source, by getting back into the cowboy sport of team roping. Once or twice a week, I'd practice for a couple of hours with some of the other local ropers at the Silver Creek Sheriff Posse arena. Most Friday nights or Saturdays throughout the summer found me competing somewhere in northern Arizona. My first published piece of writing was for *Super Looper*, the official magazine of the United States Team Roping Congress.

In the summer of 1991, my Sabbaths were interrupted when a horse fell with me, and I suffered oblique fractures at the left wrist of both the radius and ulna, chipped the navicular bone at the base of my thumb, and split my chin wide open. I preached the following Sunday with fourteen stitches in my chin and a cast to my armpit. Over the next three months, the cast kept getting progressively smaller. I cut away much of the palm of the short cast, so I could hold the bridle reins and the coils of my rope in the left hand, and got right back, literally, into the swing of things within about six weeks.

From the beginning, I took a lot of grief about

roping from a handful of church members. Rodeo cowboys have a sometimes deserved reputation of being shiftless, unfaithful drunks. Several were especially concerned that their pastor was frequently seen in the company of such vermin.

I had no one to tell how much I appreciated the unpretentious relationships I found among those men. They all called me "preacher," and though it was not my primary goal, I had ripe opportunities for ministry while hanging around the roping chutes. But just as important, my soul was refreshed. Tensions melted. Anger subsided. Worries were put into perspective. I laughed. Joy was renewed. And more times than not, I went home with a warm heart and a joyful spirit.

When I lived in the Chicago suburbs, I had a hard time finding anyone to play cowboys with me. I experimented with different ways to recharge. I ran, fished, and went for long walks on the Prairie Path trail. Today I continue to look for ways to integrate the Sabbath elements of laughter, solitude, submission, worship, and recreation into my life.

Sneaking around

You've heard the old jokes about pastors sneaking off to find a Sabbath: The golfer who told his secretary he was going to visit the Greens; the fisherman who named his boat Visitation, as in "I'll be out on Visitation for the rest of the day if anyone calls."

I'm not advocating sneakiness; it bothers me that the disapproval of a handful of cranks can make us resort to such behavior. But if people could only hear us preach with a fresh spirit, in contrast to the sermons we preach when we're chronically fatigued, perhaps we'd never again have to resort to sneakiness.

I waited for years for someone to notice and say, "Pastor, we've been watching you work, and it's making us all tired. We're so concerned about your physical and spiritual well-being that we're going to insist that you ease up enough to recharge your batteries. You can count on us to pick up the slack."

Another episode of Fantasy Island.

So I started giving that little speech to myself every week. At least the first part. And no one noticed. I couldn't believe it. I cut my workload by 20 percent, and no one complained. I still showed up when it counted, made myself visible at strategic times and places, and, most every week, preached with the passion that comes from being fresh.

5

QUESTIONS TO CHANGE A LIFE

WHEN I WAS CALLED to my previous church, some gracious folks remodeled the pastor's office. It was a spacious room, and they went all out with the fixtures: Double-pane picture windows with vertical blinds. Plush carpet. Matching walnut credenza, bookshelves, and a desk big enough to land Navy fighter jets. Color-coordinated stapler, tape dispenser, paper clip holder, and in/out trays.

My diplomas hung prominently on the wall, lest anyone wandering in should wonder about my credentials. A few comfortable chairs made it easy for people to sit back, relax, and keep Pastor Ed company.

An office is a nice place to do pastoral care and administration, but an office is no study. Accessibility desecrates a study.

So I went looking for a place to call my own. In our new sanctuary, behind the piano and up the stairs, just off the little room where candidates for baptism changed, I found that undefiled, sacred spot. An old lamp, a folding table, a chair, and an extension cord for the laptop. I was ready to get to work. It was several months before even the secretary learned the whereabouts of my secret hideaway.

There I read. I prayed. I thought and wondered. I wrote. I preached passages aloud to myself. Sometimes I even cried. Mostly, though, I asked myself a lot of questions.

Scientists need laboratories. Surgeons need operating rooms. Artists need studios. Mechanics need garages, and welders need shops. Preachers need studies. The study is a place to experiment, to grow, to mend and create, all for the medium of the sermon. Here our passion is restored as we soak in God's Word.

All professions have their instruments, tools of the trade. Ours are bound stacks of paper, filled with lines of words and few pictures. Preachers acquire books like squirrels hoard nuts, filling our nests even when we have enough to last through the winter. We try to sneak more of them into our homes, even when our spouse has laid down the law.

"What's in that bag?"

"Nothing." *Be cool, now. She can't possibly know. Don't look guilty.* "Uh, leftovers from lunch."

"There's something else in there. Did you buy another book?"

"Well, there was a sale...." It's sad, really, what we become.

My wife, Susan, won't let me read magazines or newspapers first, because I tear out illustrations and statistics, fodder for the sermon. I've stolen magazines from the doctor's office, justifying my actions by asking, *Won't this story accomplish more good in one of my sermons than moldering on this table?*

These days, though I have an office at work, my study is at home—just seven feet wide and ten feet deep. My study is both monastic retreat and prison cell. When we first looked at this house, I was able to overlook the smell of pet urine, the sight of stained, orange carpet, avocado-green wallpaper, and the filthy appliances (that could all be remedied), because I spotted a little area off the family room behind the stairs that looked like holy ground. All I needed to do was build a wall for privacy and some bookshelves.

Here, I thought, *I can meet with God, midwife sermons, and tinker with words.*

No stained glass or polished wood in this sanctuary. This is a workshop, where I keep the tools of my trade. An old metal desk holds a coffee mug full of pens, a laptop and printer, and stacks of Bibles, dictionaries, and thesauruses. Next to the desk is a 1950s-era filing cabinet, big as a bomb shelter. There my illustration files are nestled alphabetically by topic, safe from nuclear attack. Sermons are in portable files, easily rescued in case of fire.

Over on the west wall is the bookshelf, floor to ceiling. The preaching books are eye level, left side; theology on the right. Commentaries and novels are on the top shelves, notebooks and old textbooks on the bottom shelf. In case of flooding, the stuff I'd most hate to lose is up high.

Hanging around on the walls is some of my favorite junk: A bridle, a rope, a pair of spurs. A certificate for finishing Grandma's Marathon sits on the shelf in front of commentaries on the Epistles. A bulletin board I found in a dumpster holds crayoned art masterpieces by my girls and a calendar to remind me of deadlines. Fly rod, vest, and waders hang on a peg in the corner. In the opposite corner, a guitar stands ready; I only play it during my really small group of one.

I have no windows, but distractions aplenty. Just outside my door sits the television and VCR. When my two young daughters are downstairs, their choice in videos allow purple dinosaurs and dancing broccoli to wander in and say hello. About two feet from my right ear, separated only by Sheetrock, sits the piano where my wife gives lessons to second- and third-graders. Even though no one is playing right now, a halting rendition of "My Grandfather's Clock" is bouncing around in my head.

Mostly I'm in here early and late, when the girls are in bed, the TV and piano silent. The pipes rattle at me, a musty smell rises from the crawl space, but it's mine. I listen for God, pray, read, write. And I wrestle with persistent questions.

Questionable preaching

For about the last five years, I've had a 3×5 card taped to my desk with a bunch of questions on it. I ask these questions every time I preach. An airline pilot runs through a checklist before taking off; a lot of lives are at stake. I approach my task with the same idea.

Wrestling with these questions helps for several reasons. First, they simply make for a better sermon. But the biggest reason I wrestle with them each week is that they keep me from succumbing to the inherent temptations of the study.

For all my talk about my study being holy ground, it's also a wilderness of temptation. Temptations await me even before I arrive. Laziness hides behind the door, jumping on me the minute I walk through it. His twin brother Procrastination whispers, "You have plenty of time," while their evil cousin Distraction tempts me to straighten piles of books, trim my fingernails, or even clean out and organize my drawers.

But these are bush-league temptations. Concentration and the sure knowledge that Sunday is bearing down like a charging bull are usually enough to help me break free from them.

I beat off my persistent adversaries and begin another wrestling match, this time with the text. If it's a familiar passage of Scripture, I impatiently want to start throwing up walls before the foundation is completed. *Get on to the commentaries, flesh out the body of the message, find those illustrations,* whispers Hurry.

Not yet.

I read and reread the passage. If I learned one thing in my seminary preaching class, it's this: I can't open another resource until I know the big idea of the text.

The study process is like working a high school math problem; the answer is in the back of the book. Back then cheating, looking up the answer first, was useless, because the teacher wanted to see how we arrived at the answer. Cracking the commentaries too soon may give me answers, but the way I work the problem is even more important.

Get specific

So I work with the text and wrestle with my biases and with God until *I get it*. Once I've done my biblical spadework, I break for caffeine, then start in with the first question. I ask these questions every time I prepare a sermon.

1. *In one sentence, what is this sermon about?* When, on Tuesday, someone asks, "What are you preaching about Sunday?" I hope I can answer with one clear sentence. It may be similar to the big idea of the text, but it's more relevant.

I recently preached on the Lord's Prayer, using the text in Luke 11. The idea of the text was "Jesus reveals the secret of his rich prayer life." My one-sentence description of the sermon was "Prayer charges our spiritual batteries."

2. *What theological category would this fit under?* Am I being theologically faithful? If the sermon is not theological, on some level, what is it?

I once preached a Father's Day message from Psalm 15 on the characteristics of a godly man. It was biblical, but not particularly theological. If pressed, I would justify the message as illustrative of our redeemed ontological nature or some such blather.

I wish I had preached the message on Psalm 103:8–12 by Jim Nicodem in a recent issue of *Preaching Today*. It was entitled "The Father Heart of God." It was also a sermon for Father's Day, but it was a theological exploration of one aspect of the nature of God. Every father who heard it learned something about being a better dad, but the focus was Godward, not manward. Increasingly, I'm moving from the anthropocentric message toward the theocentric.

3. *What do I want my listeners to know?* This question causes my sermon to engage the mind. What information does a listener need to know before he or she can act?

In a recent sermon on forgiveness, Robert Russell, minister of Southeast Christian Church in Louisville, Kentucky, wanted his congregation to know that forgiveness will set them free from a variety of emotional and spiritual maladies. More specifically, he wanted people to know there is a reward for doing the painfully hard work of forgiveness.

4. *What do I want them to do?* This is the application question, which focuses on my listeners' hands and feet. I must be as specific and practical as possible. In Robert Russell's message, he asked specific questions not easily deflected by the heart: "What about your

boss, who denied you a raise, even though you had a more productive year than the year before? Will you forgive her? What about your dad, who left you and your mom when you were eight? Are you ready to forgive him?"

5. *What do I want them to become?* Now I'm going for the heart. What attitudes, priorities, and adjustments in lifestyle will this sermon address?

This question is often the hardest to answer, and for that reason I'm tempted to ignore it. It's easy to say, "As a result of this message, I want people to become more effective and consistent at prayer."

But what do more prayerful people look like? Will I know one when I see one? If Rick, our sound technician, put these principles of prayer to work in his life, what would he become in his work, his home, his church?

Naturally, some sermons, by nature of the text, are primarily *knowing, doing,* or *being* sermons. Yet I want to identify some element of understanding, action, and regeneration in each message I preach.

6. *How does this sermon fit with the larger vision?* This question helps me focus on the long view: How does this week's message move us toward our long-range goals? How does it fit into our church's vision statement? Am I providing this flock with a healthy, balanced diet of preaching? Is there a cohesiveness with what I've previously preached? A sense of direction?

Answer the skeptics

Sermon preparation would be a lot easier if we could just send our congregations to seminary. But since that won't happen, I have to be relevant. I have to face the pragmatism and skepticism of the age. Two questions help me do that.

So what? That is the relentless question of pragmatists: *So what if the Philistines stopped up the wells dug by Isaac's father, Abraham? I didn't sign up for a class in ancient Middle Eastern history.*

The story of Isaac and the wells in Genesis 26 has relevance for anyone who has felt the undeserved enmity of another. I heard homiletics professor Miles Jones use this text recently to call his fellow African-Americans to remove the dirt of racism from the wells of their souls. Even though they may not have initiated the racism, said the speaker, they were responsible for digging out of it. "We've got to dig *deeper*, 'cause deep won't do," became his refrain. He answered the "So what?" question beautifully.

Oh really? Many people are conditioned by life to discount every promise they hear by about 90 percent. I try to imagine the broken promises and empty assurances people have had to face: the large woman and her larger husband, for example, who for more than twenty years have tried to lose weight. Fad diets, pills, expensive health club memberships—they've been there, done that. Just last month, an infomercial *guaranteed* a revolutionary piece of exercise equipment would transform soft-and-flabby into hard-and-healthy in just minutes a day. The behemoth contraption maxed out their credit card, takes up half the family room, but hasn't taken off a pound. The woman hangs clothes on it while she's ironing.

"Oh really?" will be their reaction to a sermon entitled "Six Easy Steps to Spiritual Fitness." This question saves me from trite preaching.

Analyze my condition

Recently I attended a concert at our county fair by a country singer who has been recording hits for twenty-five years. Her band was technically precise, her gestures polished, her vocals on pitch. But as she sang, I asked myself, *How many rinky-dink fairs and rodeos has she been to over the past two and a half decades? She's not only tired, she's bored out of her mind.* After five or six of her songs, Susan and I rounded up the kids, ready to go. I'm sure the performer wished she could leave early as well. On the way home, I sang her songs with more gusto than she had. I'd hate to think of my congregation doing the same with one of my sermons.

So I wrestle with a couple more questions.

Do I believe this message will make a difference? Without this question, I could drift a long time before I'm conscious of growing cynicism or hopelessness. I can fake sincerity pretty well, but contrived passion is ugly to watch. I need to wrestle with my faith every week: faith in God, faith in the Word, faith in the foolishness of preaching.

Has this sermon made a difference in my life this week? By this stage of preparation, I've spent many hours engaging the text and thinking about its implications for life. If it has not yet touched me, dare I believe it will touch anyone else in the thirty minutes I'll be in the pulpit?

John Calvin said, "If a preacher is not first preaching to himself, better that he falls on the steps of the pulpit and breaks his neck than preaches that sermon."

Have I earnestly prayed for God to speak through me? As my friend Dennis Baker says, "Even a church service can get pretty interesting when God shows up." Have I met with him in the study? Am I expecting him to show up this Sunday?

Have I used the material of others inappropriately? Access to the sermons of great communicators is easier than ever. Plagiarism isn't just about what it takes from the person I stole it from. It's about what it does to the level of trust with those who will hear me. They may not be able to articulate this, but my listeners come with the expectation that what I'm sharing came through honest, prayerful work.

Have I tried to make myself look better than I am? Who else besides us preachers can tell stories about ourselves without getting interrupted? If I'm not careful, I can abuse the privilege and select excerpts from my life that make me look smarter, funnier, and kinder than I'll ever be.

A heart for Nick

Years ago I preached a sermon series on "Who We Are in Christ." My text for one message was Romans 8:1–2: "Therefore, there is now no condemnation for those who are in Christ Jesus, because through Christ Jesus the law of the Spirit of life set me free from the law of sin and death" (NIV).

In the study that week, I thought a lot about Nick, a recent convert, who was still held captive by a lot of destructive habits. He agonized over them, ashamed, for example, by his need for a cigarette between Sunday school and worship. I pondered the text: *What are the implications for Nick? He's come so far, but he'll have a tough time growing in Christlikeness if he's under the burden of condemnation. Lord, what can you say to him?* After several moments, other faces came to mind, and I pondered their situations as well.

Something, I don't remember what, came up that week that made me fall behind on my sermon preparation. Looking in my file from that Sunday, I preached with just a sketchy outline and this firm conviction: *Whatever else I do or don't do, I can't preach this text with even a hint of condemnation in my words, attitude, or actions.*

Sometime later Nick and I sat together at a church potluck supper. He was not a man who expressed himself well, but through a mouthful of macaroni and cheese, in a roundabout fashion, he thanked me for not hassling him about smoking. He ended his rambling with, "You're a h—— of a preacher, you know that?"

Of all the questions I agonize over during the week, the one that may be the most important is "Will my listeners know I care about them?" Love covers a multitude of pastoral sins. If my church recognizes my voice as that of a loving undershepherd, they will listen with ears of trust and faith. They'll know instinctively that I have their best interests at heart.

And there's an added benefit: They'll think I'm a better preacher than I really am.

6

PREACHING THROUGH
SPIRITUAL DROUGHT

MOST DAYS AROUND 11:45 A.M., I turn on my screen saver, grab my gym bag, and walk two blocks to SportsMed, a gym owned and operated by a local medical practice. Sue or Brenda greets me by name and hands me a locker key and a couple of towels. A few old men, their workout finished, sit at tables and argue over coffee about why Chicago winters aren't as tough as they used to be.

I change, then join the dozens already working out.

The faint strains of techno-pop come from the aerobics room, full of bouncing dancers, mostly women. The free weights are mostly unoccupied, while over at the Cybex machines, a guy who looks like the Skipper from Gilligan's Island is getting pumped up. The Schwarzenegger types don't seem to like the atmosphere here; they work out at some gym over on North Avenue called "Heavy Metal." For the most part, we in this congregation are ordinary people with lumps and limps and laproscopic scars.

Some of the people sweating around me are staff from the clinic next door: orthopedic surgeons, physical therapists, and other support personnel using their lunch hour to work out. Sans lab coats, I can't really tell the healers from the wounded.

We don't talk much, I and the lunch-time crowd, but we know each other by sight and nod, affirming one another's faithful presence. I imagine each person's story, his or her motive for being here, the dreams.

Over by the mirrors is the woman I call "the Dancer," thick through the middle, hair faded to white, gently moving her arthritic joints to a graceful heart song. A therapist with a clipboard is watching "Duck Boy" as he waddles around the track in a University of Michigan sweatshirt, dipping and pausing at each step. Fresh scars on both knees indicate his ungainly gait must be some form of therapy.

Several of the treadmills and bikes are loaded with recovering heart patients, moving slowly, but still moving. I climb on the only empty Stairmaster to warm up before I hit the weights. Next to me, "Black Widow" speaks: "Lookin' good, Doll."

Embarrassed, I stare straight ahead at the basketball court. Heavy makeup can't hide the effects of more than half a century of loneliness. She's ostensibly here on a manhunt. Every warm body with a trace of testosterone has felt her sights on his back.

Around us, on the hamster-wheel track, a guy in a full-body brace passes a creeping octogenarian jogger who looks like Walter Matthau. Nobody here but us rehab patients. Just working to reverse, or at least stave off, the inevitable effects of illness and inactivity.

I came to this place over a year ago with one goal—to make sweeping changes in the way I look. In my mind, I'm still as lean and athletic as I was at eighteen. But one look in the mirror betrays that sentimental image—the occupational hazards of adulthood have inflated and softened me.

I had other needs: A few flights of stairs would put me into a heart-pounding sweat. Too many hours in a chair had tightened my hamstrings and lower back to the point of chronic pain. *Enough of this nonsense*, I thought. *A few weeks of work in the gym and I'll be back in shape.*

My goals? Simple: To regain the appearance of my youth.

I've been working out faithfully for over a year now. I lift weights three times a week. I run or get some other form of aerobic exercise at least three other days. There's no question I'm enjoying myself. But am I making progress?

When I look at my fellow gym rats, I have to say I don't notice much, if any, change in the way *any of us* look, though we're here most every day. At least for me, the scale offers scant encouragement. My weight is still on the wrong side of 200. The mirror? At home, I never look in a mirror until after my shower when I wipe away just enough condensation to shave and comb my hair. But at the gym, wall-to-wall mirrors function like the Word of God held before me, my sins revealed in panoramic view.

If no one is watching, I flex my pecs or biceps, looking hopefully for evidence of growth. Some days I even start to believe I'm making progress, but most days I head for the showers, trying to reestablish faith in the power of exercise by muttering my mantra, "No deposit, no return."

Is it worth the sacrifice when there is so little visible payoff? The cost of my membership strains our family budget. Taking this midday break means I must come to work early or stay late.

But still I come, and the question is *why?*

Inevitable slump

The apostle Paul told Timothy, "For physical training is of some value, but godliness has value for all things, holding promise for both the present life and the life to come" (1 Tim. 4:8, NIV). If godliness is of value for all things, then surely preaching is included. Shouldn't training in godliness be just the thing to improve my preaching?

Several years ago, I heard of a seminary classmate who prefaced his sermon with a public apology. He acknowledged that the previous week's sermon had been especially atrocious, then offered this by way of explanation: "Usually, just before I come into the sanctuary to begin the service, I pray in my study. Last week I didn't take the time to pray. Please forgive me." He went on to deliver a message that he assured his congregation was undergirded by much prayer, but I heard it was still pretty bad. The person who told me this story suspected his lack of the preaching gift was a more plausible explanation than his lack of prayer. I have never revealed my superstitions about prayer and sermon preparation with my congregation, but I'm quite familiar with the expectation of my acquaintance.

Too often preachers may feel the necessity of spiritual disciplines, not as a means of drawing closer to God, but as sermon insurance. A long week, too little sleep, and too much tension cramp my study time, so I compensate by praying fervently, asking that God bless my message anyway. I can think, *If I pray well, journal well, memorize Scripture well, the sermon will go well. If the sermon flops, I must not have done enough of the spiritual stuff.*

Is that true?

In examining almost ten years of journaling, I can't find consistent evidence proving that periods of spiritual vitality are directly correlated with sermonic excellence. If anything, they seem inversely related. I've preached some of the most fruitful messages of my life during spiritual droughts—periods of virtual prayerlessness. What am I supposed to do with *that* horrifying discovery? I hate the overriding sense of hypocrisy I feel when I deliver bold messages with a withering spirit.

I've discovered two types of sermon slumps, one visible to all, the other identifiable only by me.

About five years ago, I went through a six-month streak where every message seemed on target. But I was struggling with a lack of consistency in the spiritual disciplines, complicated by discouragement with some church conflict that refused to die. During that time, a friend and I were shingling his house. He kept talking about how he was shifting some major priorities in his life as a result of my last several sermons. Normally taciturn, on the roof that day he couldn't keep quiet. The spiritual growth and confidence in God he was experiencing—*that he claimed was a direct result of my preaching*—was exactly what I was lacking. *How could this be?* I prayed. *Lord, how can you give him something through me without me being affected by it as well?*

This slump was internal, the result of spiritual entropy. I was the primary casualty.

On the other hand, I've also gone through a couple of sermon slumps, some short, some long, while in rich relationship with my Father. In early 1994 I was laboring through a series of messages, each focused on the *hamartia*, the fatal flaw of various Old Testament leaders, even as I was experiencing depth in my prayer time. In the midst of that slump, I attended a week-long retreat for pastors that continues to be a significant signpost in my spiritual journey. I returned home with an even deeper spiritual passion, yet for weeks I struggled to find my balance in the pulpit. Relief came only when I abandoned the series that I had lost interest in and started preaching from the Gospel passages that were engaging me every morning in my quiet time.

That second slump began internally but ended up external—my lack of interest resulted in lazy study habits—and the congregation suffered the consequences.

Experiences like these have led me to explore further the relationship between spiritual vitality and passionate preaching. I never think of abandoning preaching when vitality is high. But when vitality is low, I ask myself, *Is it hypocrisy to continue to preach with conviction during times of soul drought? By managing appearances, am I being deceptive?*

If faith is the substance of things hoped for, the evidence of things not seen, then preaching provides me the perfect opportunity to grow in faith. When preaching well while feeling spiritually anemic, I can now see this as God at work in me. When preaching poorly, I place faith in the hope that God is at work making a difference in *other* people's lives, even when I've failed to communicate well. Preaching, then, is an act of faith either way.

Scripture gives ample evidence that Paul was a strong preacher, and no one can doubt his calling to preach. One affirmation of his calling came right after arriving in Corinth, when God told Paul in a vision, "Do not be afraid; keep on speaking, do not be silent. For I am with you" (Acts 18:9–10, NIV).

But the Corinthians were less than impressed. Paul acknowledged their stinging appraisal in 2 Corinthians 10:10: "For some say, 'His letters are weighty and forceful, but in person he is unimpressive and his speaking amounts to nothing'" (NIV).

In one form or another, what preacher hasn't heard that criticism?

Perhaps he simply paled in comparison to Apollos, who had wowed the crowd with his rhetoric. Maybe Paul was in a major-league preaching slump during at least part of his stay in Corinth. First Corinthians 2:4–5 reads, "My message and my preaching were not with wise and persuasive words, but with a demonstration of the Spirit's power, so that your faith might not rest on men's wisdom, but on God's power."

Sounds to me like the words of a man who found God faithful even in the midst of a preaching slump. How encouraging to know that even when my sermons are not as wise and persuasive as I'd hoped, God's power will still be manifested through his Holy Spirit!

Frequently someone has thanked me for saying something in a sermon that "made a real difference in my life." I appreciate such compliments. But sometimes I didn't say what she said I said. I didn't say anything close to what she said I said. But somehow, the Spirit spoke to her in spite of what I was saying. If such conversations happened frequently, I'd be tempted to forget preparation and just show up on Sunday, ready to wing it for the Lord. But I've been unable to control these experiences, or make the

Spirit appear on cue. The Spirit works at God's discretion.

It appears the Spirit is at work in me and through me whether or not I'm having my quiet time.

I have a friend who has been given powerful gifts of communication. He delivers messages in a way people inevitably describe as *anointed*. In just about any context, his preaching dramatically touches people's lives. His church is often recognized by his denomination for evangelistic growth. He is invited to speak at large gatherings.

Yet he admitted to me once, during a time of uncharacteristic vulnerability, that the only time he prays is in the course of performing his pastoral duties. He said he has struggled to break out of that deficit for over twenty years.

I worry about how his spiritual void makes him vulnerable to temptation. He has come dangerously close on two occasions to compromising his integrity.

I also know a pastor who probably spends more than two hours a day, every day, in prayer. He regularly finds time for solitude and silence. He has committed large portions of the Bible to memory. His heart breaks for the hurting and needy. Yet those left in his dying church are ready to fire him, in part because he does not appear to possess the gifts of teaching and preaching. Both of my friends appear headed for tragic circumstances; both sophist and saint could meet with dismissal from ministry.

Many preachers, unfortunately, could side with

my friends. Those gifted at communicating always live with the nagging suspicion they can get along pretty good without spiritual depth; the spiritually sensitive may believe they can be effective without good communication skills. Neither are true, and both inevitably hurt both preacher and congregation. Those of us somewhere in the middle are in even worse shape, for we wrestle daily with *both* temptations.

So let me ask a question that borders on sacrilege: If effective preaching is primarily the result of spiritual giftedness and the anointing of the Holy Spirit, if fervent prayer and daily adherence has little visible effect on my preaching, and if no one else will notice, why pursue spiritual fitness?

Why work out?

My faith heritage has trained me to avoid questioning such inconsistencies and merely apply the theology of Nike: *Just Do It*. We're commanded by the Scriptures: "Flee the evil desires of youth, and pursue righteousness, faith, love and peace, along with those who call on the Lord out of a pure heart" (2 Tim. 2:22, NIV).

So *Just Do It*. "Set an example for the believers in speech, in life, in love, in faith and in purity (1 Tim. 4:12b, NIV).

That's not the worst way to respond to the authority of Scripture. In fact, it's the starting point.

Obedience leads to righteousness, claims Paul. But how much more motivated is the one who understands the reasoning behind the order?

I spent four years in the U.S. Air Force. The it's-not-just-a-job-it's-an-adventure began in San Antonio, Texas, with basic training. Part of the genius of building a cohesive military unit is to dress everyone in fatigues and cut off all their hair. No longer were we black or white, we were all green. After the barber got hold of us, the rednecks, the hippies, and the pretty boys all looked alike.

We learned to obey the drill instructor without question. The reason for this is obvious: When someone screams, "Down!" those who stand around to argue or offer alternative suggestions are riddled with bullets.

But we didn't start learning obedience on the combat course with bullets; we started with underwear.

Specifically, on day two we learned to fold our underwear and T-shirts into perfect six-inch squares. We did this because our drill instructor said so. No other reason needed. Come inspection time, woe to the man whose underwear measured six by six and one-eighth. It would be better for him if a millstone were tied around his neck and he were forced to listen to the all-night Barry Manilow radio-fest. But I digress.

If you disobeyed, you reaped the consequences. The old military saw goes, "Ours is not to question 'Why?' Ours is but to do or die." Blind obedience. It must be learned before it can be improved upon. Once a person has completed basic training, though, he is thrust into a modern military environment that is quite different from basic training.

That's because supervisors aren't sent to the same schools as drill instructors. Supervisors don't rely on the same box of tools as drill instructors. As a young sergeant, I received training in how to build unified teams in order to carry out the necessary tasks to reach our desired objective. That's a far more effective strategy for empowering a fighting force than the constant threat of court-martial for insubordination.

The reason for the different emphasis?

Obedience and discipline are enhanced when they stem from *want-to*, not *have-to*. That insight into human nature did not come courtesy of Uncle Sam; it comes from a God who created us that we might partner with him willingly to accomplish kingdom purposes.

The want-to

The Nike philosophy works for rookies. But we old-timers need Paul's philosophy:

> I want to know Christ and the power of his resurrection and the fellowship of sharing in his sufferings, becoming like him in his death, and so, somehow, to attain to the resurrection from the dead. Not that I have already ob-

tained all this, or have already been made perfect, but I press on to take hold of that for which Christ Jesus took hold of me. Brothers, I do not consider myself yet to have taken hold of it. But one thing I do: Forgetting what is behind and straining toward what is ahead, I press on toward the goal to win the prize for which God has called me heavenward in Christ Jesus. (Phil. 3:10–14, NIV)

I *want* to know Christ.

No matter how effective my preaching might be for others, without knowing the love and warmth of Christ, the ice crystallized around my heart will bring hypothermia to my soul. Unless I know the power of his resurrection, cynicism overwhelms compassion. I start to believe that, given a choice, people will make the wrong one every time. Even if I communicate well, I preach as one without hope.

Weddings become merely the prelude to divorce court. Holy Week becomes a crushing season of duty. I tend to view the twice-a-year crowd as shallow consumers unworthy of my best presentation of our hope in Christ.

I *want* to know Christ.

Without sharing in the fellowship of his suffering, I can't hope to survive the inevitable conflicts of pastoral ministry. Most of us would stand with courage and conviction before a firing squad before renouncing our faith. Yet the unrelenting shallowness of most congregational conflict and criticism rubs blisters on our souls until we either limp away in pain, or, over time, develop callouses to protect our vulnerable spots. Callouses ease the pain, but they rob us of the sensitivity needed to feel and respond to the hurt and insecurity behind most congregational conflict. Preaching takes on a harshness. Proclaiming truth, yes—but truth without sensitivity, not knowing or caring why our people bicker so.

I *want* to know Christ.

Without forging ahead, eyes focused on the heavenly prize, my ever-present temptation to compromise my message becomes too much. I begin grinding away the rough edges of the gospel to make it comfortably fit contemporary life, instead of grinding away the excesses of contemporary life until it fits the gospel. I avoid speaking to topics that offend, especially those that might offend our most generous givers. The desire to please my church overrides the desire to please Christ.

These are the sins of the prayerless preacher: cynicism, callousness, and compromise. They render our sermons impotent even when well-communicated.

I *want* to know Christ.

Without sitting at the feet of Christ daily, I can try to *look* like him without *becoming* like him. A certain tone of voice in the pastoral prayer, a concerned look, a knowing nod when others mention matters of depth—these are enough to make most people believe I've got the real thing. The ecclesiastical equivalent to a double-head-fake allows me to admit to spiritual struggles, knowing that most people will believe I'm just being modest. Nothing is easier to caricature than a preacher, and nothing is harder to build than the character of a preacher. No wonder some preachers go for style over substance.

The unpleasant reality is most listeners will never know if I've got the real thing. But I know. I've never been able to fool myself. That knowledge keeps me going even when I don't have the want-to. I hate faking it.

Internal rewards

After a long, hard year of faithful exercise, not one person has commented, "Wow, where'd you get those muscles?" Yet I still work out faithfully. In spite of little visual confirmation, I know something is going on within me that scales and mirrors cannot validate.

Am I making progress? Without question.

My stamina is up, no doubt about that. I've shoveled enough snow this winter to bring on a dozen heart attacks, with not even a sore back. I can take the several flights of stairs from my office to the fax machines two at a time. My latest fitness evaluation showed my body-fat percentage was down and my flexibility, strength, and endurance much improved. And it has been a long time since I've had insomnia. I've come through another gray, dreary Chicago winter with only nips and growls from the dark dog of depression that haunts transplants like me who grew up accustomed to sunshine.

Those are all great benefits; they simply are not the results I most expected and wanted.

I *want* to know Christ, not because it makes me preach better, but because it allows me to preach with integrity. It allows me to preach with hope. With a sensitive heart and with conviction. And that's better than preaching better.

7

PRAYERS FOR INTERVENTION

"YOU WANT TO MEET after this and pray together?" whispered the old man.

I nodded, unable to look at him, and choked down the lump in my throat. We were sitting in the Monday afternoon staff meeting of a large suburban church. I was pastor of the new church plant sponsored by this congregation. Dr. Hunker, after more than forty years as a missionary in Taiwan, was pastor of the Chinese congregation. Both of us were ancillary to most of the discussion taking place.

The senior pastor had asked for prayer requests. My pride and reputation were on the line, but I felt compelled to ask for prayer for several things, starting with a minor health concern and working my way up to the biggie—my preaching, which was not being well-received by the nucleus of people joining me in the startup effort from this sponsoring church. My core group was used to hearing a pulpit master; I was just a rookie.

That day I was looking for more than advice on how to improve my sermons; I desperately needed some acceptance apart from my preaching.

But after hearing the first half of a sentence of my request, the senior pastor cut me off, asked for other prayer requests in a tone that signaled we had enough on the table, offered a brief, generic prayer, then moved on to the business at hand.

The lesson of that day came later, as Dr. Hunker and I left the air-conditioned bustle of the conference room for the warm quiet of his study. From under the worn couch, he pulled a couple of straw mats, each broken down in two spots from someone's faithful knees. We knelt together without a word, he placed his hands on my head, and for the next forty-five minutes, prayed for me with an intensity and passion I can feel to this day. (A year later, as I knelt for the laying on of hands during my ordination, I immediately recognized the touch of Dr. Hunker, even before he began to pray for me.)

That afternoon in his study, he prayed for my health, my marriage, our soon-to-be-born child, and all my worries and insecurities. Just when I thought he had covered everything, he moved on to the big stuff—that I would have a passion for God, a passion for souls, and a passion for preaching. I cannot remember specific words, but I can still sense his patriarchal blessing, and the presence of God that surrounded me as that faithful servant soaked my needy heart in the warmth of grace.

After most of an hour was past, he was done. I blew my nose and wiped my face dry, then Dr. Hunker sat with me and talked frankly about spiritual warfare and the role of prayer, specifically praise and worship, in standing strong in the fight. I'm sure my jaw dropped at some of the stories he told of confrontations with darkness throughout his ministry. Perhaps I thought, *Maybe in Taiwan. But I doubt I'll encounter anything like this in my ministry.*

I didn't know then that that afternoon would be a watershed event in my life and my ministry.

Earlier I discussed the role of the spiritual disciplines and their relationship to preaching. For too long, I pursued them merely as sermon insurance. I don't think the average person in the pew can tell by the quality of a sermon whether the preacher prayed as part of preparation, and in some cases, neither can the preacher. But the spiritual disciplines *are* an effective measure of the preacher's passion, which may or may not be visible.

Prayer, for me, is a gauge of what I believe in, a confirmation of what I consider vital, an indication of where my passion lies. I seldom pray about things unimportant to me. I've never prayed to own a water-skiing boat. I never learned to water-ski, mainly because I'm scared to death of deep water. And I really don't worry about the hiccups in the stock market; I keep my money invested in groceries and clothes for the kids. I never pray for things I don't believe in, either. I've never prayed that I might see a UFO. Never prayed for the safety of professional wrestlers. Never once prayed for a World Series victory for the Chicago Cubs.

But I pray daily, with passion, for my family's physical, emotional, and spiritual needs. I pray fervently about my work writing and editing publications for pastors and church leaders. These things are life to me.

In the same way, an urgency to pray throughout the sermon process tells me, at least on one level, that I still believe in preaching. And it signals to me that I really care about the outcome of the message in the lives of the people to whom I preach.

Preparatory prayer

I've always preferred to start the sermon as early in the week as possible to let it simmer within for as long as possible. Monday morning isn't too soon to begin grappling with and praying through the text: *What did it mean then? What does it mean now? Dear God, help me understand!*

A church directory sat on my desk with my Bible. I thumbed through it, a couple of pages a day, and prayed for the families of our church every week: *Where do they hurt? Where do they doubt? Why, Father, are they struggling so? Use this message to be a part of the solution to their deepest needs.*

Sometimes when communication fails it is because something went wrong with the sender. But other times, communication fails because of the inability of the receiver to *hear* the message—like receiving a phone call from someone who can hear you but you can only say, "Call me back. I can barely hear you."

The prophet Jeremiah described his audience like this: "To whom can I speak and give warning? Who will listen to me? Their ears are closed so they cannot hear. The word of the Lord is offensive to them; they find no pleasure in it. But I am full of the wrath of the Lord, and I cannot hold it in" (Jer. 6:10–11).

Maybe I've read too many Frank Peretti novels, or maybe it's just that the unseen realm of darkness and light has begun to come into focus, but I've become increasingly sensitive to the significance of prayer to create a teaching environment in which people are freed from the influence of the Father of Lies.

My enlightenment began when I was called as pastor of a church in a community that was more than 70 percent Mormon. The beautiful 100-year-old ward house (church) was the literal and symbolic center of town. Every street name was based on its relationship to the church. We lived on 372 South First Street East, not to be confused with 372 East First Street South, in accordance with Brigham Young's "Plan of Zion."

Joseph Smith, founder of The Church of Jesus Christ of Latter-day Saints, was heavily influenced by different occultic practices of his time, and the ritual and doctrine of his followers today reflect that heritage. In addition to the Mormon influence, we were bordered not too far to the north and south by two Indian reservations, where mystic Native American religions have taken on new life in the past few years, in part fueled by New Age seekers. To our immediate east lay some cheap land that was subdivided into forty-acre "ranches" back in the '70s. This remote region became not only a haven for retirees who wanted a little place in the country but also a hiding place for survivalists, militias, child molesters, drug lab operators, cultural dropouts from the '60s, New Age practitioners, and more than a few small communes reminiscent of David Koresh and Waco, Texas.

It was, in many ways, the antithesis of Wheaton, Illinois, where I lived while working at LEADERSHIP.

In the diverse context of rural Arizona, we sought to evangelize and make disciples. We immediately collided with people and circumstances outside the normal range of conflict common to most churches. I found Neil Anderson's books, including *The Bondage Breaker* and *Victory Over the Darkness* immensely helpful both in understanding our situation and in learning how to administer pastoral care.[1]

Over the next several years in that ministry, some people found victory over addictions. Others renounced involvement with false religions and occultic practices, and confessed Jesus Christ as the Way, the Truth, and the Life. Still others found freedom from shameful memories that had kept them in chains for years.

And yet others chose darkness over light.

[1]Neil T. Anderson, *The Bondage Breaker* (Eugene, Ore.: Harvest House Publishers, 1993). Neil T. Anderson, *Victory Over Darkness* (Ventura, Calif.: Regal Books, 1990).

Even within the fellowship of our church, we experienced spiritual attack. I found some who were literally unable to hear God's Word proclaimed. My voice was just one of several voices shouting for attention in their heads.

Beyond the evidence of spiritual darkness in the lives of people who considered themselves believers, there was physical evidence of some kind of bizarre, ritualistic activity around our church facility. For example, on three occasions I arrived at the church on a Sunday morning to find blood of some kind smeared over the front doors. Once, a dead cat was wedged between the door handles. I usually arrived around 6 A.M., so I managed to clean the mess up before anyone else arrived. Maybe it was just kids playing pranks—maybe it was something else.

Then there was the morning after a full moon, when I walked into our sanctuary and discovered the side door had been left ajar just enough so that the lock did not catch. On the carpet in front of the communion table was the matted hair of some kind of animal. Maybe a shedding dog just wandered in and took a little nap—maybe it was something else.

I still hesitate to speculate about how to interpret such physical evidence, for I'm not inclined to see a demon behind every sneeze. But the occultic environment in which we ministered, the spiritual bondage of some in our midst, and this recurring weirdness had the effect of scaring me enough that I began to pray with a fervor I've not had before or since.

119

When I looked at my church's needs as a lack of information, I was confident I could enlighten them out of my education and communication skills. When I looked at their needs as primarily emotional, I could put on my counselor's hat. It was only when I began to see the dysfunction of our church and the community as stemming from our depraved nature, a sin-tainted world, and the ongoing influence of the Prince of Darkness—and only when I came to an utter lack of hope in anything other than God's direct intervention—that I began to pray with new passion.

So it came to pass that prayer and sermon preparation became, for me, inseparably intertwined. I know that God does not dwell in a temple, yet our sanctuary became a holy place for me every day throughout the week. During the daytime, as sunlight through the glass made dancing dust motes visible, God's presence strengthened and brightened me. At night, the shadow and contrast made me ever more sensitive to the reality of another realm beyond my sight.

I became utterly desperate, absolutely convinced that I, my friends, my church, and my family were without hope unless God directly intervened. The only posture suitable for such prayer was spread-eagle prostrate on the floor. When I recall what happened there on the floor, I find I lack the freedom to describe it in detail. I would no more give details of that time alone with God than I would describe my physical relationship with my wife. I can't write or talk of it and retain any of the sanctity of the event.

But in those hours, day by day, God sustained me, empowered me, and renewed me to preach with hope and passion.

Pre-game prayer

Inevitably, Saturday night came, and Sunday would follow quickly on its heels. After putting the kids to bed, I would often walk the three short blocks to the church to wage war. In Paul's rich description of spiritual war, he said, "Put on the full armor of God so that you can take your stand against the devil's schemes. For our struggle is not against flesh and blood, but against the rulers, against the authorities, against the powers of this dark world and against the spiritual forces of evil in the heavenly realms" (Eph. 6:11–12, NIV).

I entered the sanctuary singing psalms, hymns, and spiritual songs at the top of my lungs. I reasoned the spiritual forces of evil would flee in the face of earnest praise to God.

"May God arise, may his enemies be scattered," I sang, making up the tune as I went along. "May his foes flee before him. . . . Sing to God, sing praise to his name, extol him who rides on the clouds—his name is the Lord" (Ps. 68:1, 4, NIV).

I would then stand in every doorway, my hands on the threshold, praying aloud that all people who passed through would be freed from the distractions and lies that had held them captive. "You will know the truth, and the truth will set you free" (John 8:32, NLT).

I then walked the length of every pew, praying for the people who predictably sat there week after week. I prayed for troubled homes, rebellious teens, and crippled marriages. I'd pause at the usual seat of the Mormon alcoholic husband of one of our members, praying for freedom over his addiction and spiritual bondage. Over there, left side, near the front, sat Jerry, the professional skeptic, who continued to attend semi-regularly despite his insistent doubts. Fred, my most vocal critic, sat near the back and sighed loudly whenever he felt I said something stupid (almost every other sentence). I'd pray for him that, in spite of my stupidity, he could somehow hear a word from God. While I was praying, the sermon I had prepared in the study percolated through my brain and into my soul. I sought supernatural connections between God's Word and the occupants of each seat.

After working through the pews, I'd visit the sound booth, microphones, and musical instruments—the dwelling places for demons of the most hideous kind. Then on to the pulpit, where I asked the Lord to give me courage and conviction, clarity of thought, and a heightened sensitivity to his Spirit during the actual delivery of the message. I completed the Saturday night ritual by asking that the pulpit, a mere piece of wood, be consecrated as an altar upon which I sacrificed, yet again, my pride, ambition, and desire to be liked. Early the next morning, I'd come once again for a brief time of prayer before turning on lights and the furnace, making sure the bulletins were out, and picking up empty beer cans in the parking lot.

My secretary had given me a collection of Puritan prayers, published by Banner of Truth Trust, entitled *The Valley of Vision*, one of my prized possessions. One prayer, "A Minister's Preaching," I still carry in my Bible. It was more often than not my Sunday morning, pre-preaching prayer:

My Master God,
I am desired to preach today,
    but go weak and needy to my task;
Yet I long that people might be
    edified with divine truth,
    that an honest testimony
    might be borne for thee.
Give me assistance
    in preaching and prayer,
    with heart uplifted
    for grace and unction.
Present to my view
    things pertinent to my subject,
    with fullness of matter
    and clarity of thought,
    proper expressions, fluency, fervency,
    a feeling sense of the things I preach,
    and grace to apply them

to men's consciences.
Keep me conscious all the while
of my defects,
and let me not gloat in pride
over my performance.
Help me to offer a testimony
for thyself,
and to leave sinners inexcusable
in neglecting thy mercy.
Give me freedom to open the sorrows
of thy people,
and to set before them
comforting considerations.
Attend with power the truth preached,
and awaken the attention
of my slothful audience.
May thy people be refreshed,
melted, convicted, comforted,
and help me to use the strongest
arguments drawn from Christ's
incarnation and sufferings,
that men might be made holy.
I myself need thy support,
comfort, strength, holiness,
that I might be a pure channel
of thy grace,
and be able to do
something for thee;
Give me, then, refreshment
among thy people,

and help me not to treat
excellent matter
in a defective way,
or bear a broken testimony
to so worthy a redeemer,
or be harsh in treating
of Christ's death,
its design and end,
from lack of warmth and fervency.
And keep me in tune with thee
as I do this work.
Amen.[2]

Post-game prayer

Just a few weeks ago, I preached in a Baptist church where the tradition of the altar call is alive and well. My text was Philippians 3:5–11. My title: "Life's Most Difficult Choice." The point: "Life's greatest satisfaction is not found in our success (vv. 5–6), our righteousness (v. 9), or our comfort (vv. 10–11), but is instead found in the intimacy of knowing Christ. My life's theme—expressed in that key phrase, I *want* to know Christ—became our refrain. Not *have* to. I *want* to know Christ.

I closed the message by encouraging people to consider ways they had allowed the search for success, self-righteousness, or personal comfort to edge out

___
[2]Arthur Bennett, *Valley of Vision* (Carlisle, Pa.: Banner of Truth, 1975).

the search for intimacy with Christ: "Let me encourage you to pray silently, asking God to reveal the answers to your heart-searching questions. And I'll be standing here at the front if you'd like someone to pray with you or have questions."

As the pianist began playing quietly, a businessman in a suit that cost more than my truck immediately strode up the aisle and grabbed my hand in a double-fisted grip. "I can't believe I've allowed it to happen," he said, his voice growing rough. "I really love the Lord, but over the past year or so I've started a new job. I've tried so hard to get a handle on it that I've given what belongs to Christ to my job. Would you pray for me, that I can re-prioritize my life, and that I'll be paying attention so that it never happens again?"

We did pray—first me, then him. He thanked me and returned to his seat.

Afterward I was shaking hands, and the man who had responded came through and thanked me again. "I don't know why that decision had to be made publicly," he said. "But thanks for giving me the opportunity to step out. I really needed that."

I don't often see such immediate results from a sermon, but when I do, my passion for what God has called me to do re-ignites. I redouble my efforts to implement the spiritual disciplines and, specifically, to pray—to pray for the war God is waging through the sermon.

8

PREDESTINED
COMPULSION

WHEN RANCHERS IN CATRON COUNTY, New Mexico, lost livestock due to predators, they made a phone call, and old Bill Blue, government trapper, was dispatched to take care of the felonious varmints. Bill was a twentieth-century mountain man who had never seen the movie *Bambi*, so he lost no sleep over his controversial role in maintaining the balance of predator and prey.

Bill had a couple of nasty dogs who helped him bring murdering coyotes and mountain lions to justice. Butch was from of some indeterminate hound stock, one ear nearly gone from a long-ago brawl. It was fitting that this dog had a government job; he was surly and had a general disdain for all living creatures.

Bill called his other mutt Princess. Crusty old trappers don't usually give dogs, even girl dogs, such prissy names. True, she had a better personality than Butch, but she was evidently the kind of princess from days of yore when royalty bathed on a biannual basis.

One day I saw Bill parking his old Chevy Apache pickup at the grocery store. Butch was riding in the back, standing on the spare tire, hackles raised, growling at some little kid, who started to cry. The mother's eyes were watering, not from fear, but from the odor of scent bait wafting from Bill's trapping truck.

In spite of his olfactory repugnance, I liked the old man, so I walked over to say hello. Princess was sitting proudly in the pickup cab. She really didn't even look like a dog at first glance. She most closely resembled a sheep whose wool had been partially melted in a horrible chemical spill.

After shaking hands, I commented, "You sure think a lot of that old dog, don't you, Bill?"

"Well now, I guess I do. But that's my business, ain't it?"

"Where'd she get that name, Bill?" I pressed. "She doesn't look like any princess I've seen."

"Don't give me none of yer bull, young feller," he warned. "What I name my dogs is also my own business."

"I'm not makin' fun, Bill," I told him, backing off. "I'm real curious."

Bill worked his chew of tobacco around, then spit while squinting at me, trying to ascertain the purity of my motive.

"Wull, if you really wanna know, I found her 'bout six years ago, when I was workin' the old Cleveland ranch near Datil. Caught her in a trap. Funniest lookin' mutt I ever seen. Her fur was clipped short, 'cept for her ears and a ball on the end of her tail.

Some idiot had tied pink ribbons in her hair and even painted her toenails.

"I knew she was some old lady's lap dog, but we was twenty-five miles from the nearest house. Where she come from I never found out. I put up a notice at the Eagles Guest Ranch bar, but nobody ever claimed her. So I kept her."

Bill was a reader, so on his next trip to the bookmobile that serviced our remote part of the world, he picked up a dog book in addition to his usual load of Zane Grey and Louis L'Amour paperbacks.

"Found out she was a standard poodle, bred to hunt back in the old country. But fer the last hundred years, people been showin' these dogs fer their looks. He paused and gave her a warm look. You can't tell it now, but she was ugly as sin when I found 'er. I let her fur grow out normal, and you can see now how she might win one of them shows."

Actually, I couldn't, but he went on with his story.

"Anyway, I decided to see if she'd still hunt. Took to it like a coon takes to roastin' ears. She runs on instinct, you can't train a dog to think the way she does. Well, wasn't long till she was makin' ol' Butch look bad. I reckon that's why he's so dang cranky. Anyway, I decided she needed a special handle, so I thunk up the snobbiest durn name I could think of. Yessir, when she goes to work on a track, you know she was born and bred to it. It's her royal bloodline. That's my Princess."

Embarrassed by his openness, Bill reached in the

open window of the truck and rubbed her head. Princess sighed, resting contentedly under his hand. I still thought she was seriously lacking in personal hygiene, but I had to admit I was looking at a rare creature—one who had found the purpose for which she was created. Freed to follow her instincts, she enjoyed the love and respect of the one who had rescued her from a life where appearance mattered more than purpose.

Pride buster

For those so called, preaching fulfills the purpose for which they were created. Paul wrote, "When I preach the gospel, I cannot boast, for I am compelled to preach. Woe to me if I do not preach the gospel!" (1 Cor. 9:16, NIV). Preaching *is* compulsive behavior for those bred for it. After a couple of weeks away from the pulpit, preachers become anxious. I know preachers who plan their vacations around the chance to preach in someone else's pulpit.

It's almost impossible for me to read any passage of the Bible without thinking of homiletical possibilities. I can't read a newspaper, book, or magazine without a pen or scissors in hand to mark or cut out illustrations and quotes. While editor of *Preaching Today*, I got paid to listen to some of the best sermons in North America. I found my work, in one sense, frustrating. Listening to great sermons made me want to preach great sermons. Gratefully, most Sundays I was able to pinch-hit in local pulpits.

Trying to trace my compulsion back to its source has been a revelation to me. I began by exploring all the carnal sources. I have no illusion about the purity of my motives to preach. Most likely, I reasoned, my compulsion to preach originated out of pride. Indeed, some Sundays I felt, briefly, something like pride following the delivery of a message. But those moments are always followed by a painful memory that pinches back its growth—my rookie year of preaching.

At the time, I was still in seminary, involved in a church plant in an affluent suburb of a midwestern city and quite puffed up by this opportunity of a life-time. My undergraduate work had been in communications. I knew the theories of dialectic. I understood the principles of rhetoric. Several years in a sales position had given me confidence and real-world experience. My professors and denominational leaders made a big fuss, and I was convinced that I would be the next big name on the homiletical hot-air circuit.

I wanted to begin that ministry on the best possible foot, so I determined to preach a sermon that had received rave reviews (in its written form) from my preaching professor. Its numerous quotes and illustrations from great literature and dead philosophers seemed ideally suited for what I perceived to be a highly literate, educated congregation. Nervous, yet thrilled, I delivered. Surely there had never been a sermon on that text, that topic so brilliantly inspired, diligently prepared, and skillfully executed.

Back at school, I gave a glowing report to my class-mates. "I wowed them," I said. "Anyone who couldn't hit a home run to a congregation like that shouldn't be preaching."

But at staff meeting the next Wednesday, the pastor of the sponsoring church gently informed me that he had received a number of calls, begging that I not be asked back. The reason? My preaching. They didn't like it: No one could hear me, and what they did hear was dry and boring.

The pastor told me, "Look. It's not fair to judge anyone on only one sermon. These folks have ex-tremely high expectations, but I think you can get a lot better in a hurry. We'll give you another month and see how it works out."

I couldn't have been more surprised if I'd learned that Billy Graham had just gotten saved. Surely my initial reaction couldn't have been that far off. I tried to remember why I'd felt so good after the sermon. Was it simply my relief to be done? What had gone wrong?

I had only the vaguest sense that I'd not quite con-nected with the congregation, but blamed it on the room conditions. We were meeting in an elementary school multipurpose room, and the sound and space were not well-suited for preaching.

But the evidence said *I* was the problem. No use arguing about it. I could step up to the challenge—or choke. That next Sunday, seen through the lens of fear, every congregant seemed to me to have pursed lips and crossed arms. They didn't want me there; I didn't want to be there. I didn't think God wanted to be there that morning.

I stepped to the pulpit. I felt pretty passionate about the text and tried to let it be known. I projected my tenor voice as best I could. I cut back on the literary illustrations and even managed to get a modest laugh out of one story. Following the closing prayer, I felt like a bull rider again—just glad to be alive. After shaking hands with a number of people, who seemed somewhat warmer, I was starting to relax when a big guy in an expensive sweater walked up and stuck a bulletin covered with scribbles into my hands.

"Do you plan on doing this for the rest of your life?" he demanded.

"Uh, what do you mean? Preach?"

"If that's what you want to call it. Listen, I make a good living as a motivational speaker, and if you want to make it as a communicator, you've got to learn some things."

"Like what?"

"Like what I wrote here. I counted at least nine cardinal rules of effective speaking that you violated today."

I looked at the paper, trembling in my hands. No one had ever told me about nine cardinal rules. I wondered if they came down from Sinai with Moses or from Dallas by way of Zig Ziglar.

"Look," he said, softening only a bit. "You've obviously studied your Bible, but that won't cut it unless you connect with people." He briefly walked me through the list, explaining each point. The final one was this:

"What was that reference to *Moby Dick* about? No one here has read Melville since college. We read stuff like *Sports Illustrated* and watch stupid TV sitcoms like *Roseanne*. When was the last time *you* read *Moby Dick*?"

(Well, counting the time I lifted the story from some ancient tome of *Modern Sermon Illustrations* in the seminary library, never.)

He continued, "You need to relate to where we are. But we need to relate to you as well. You haven't told us one thing about yourself; not one illustration came from your life. Have you got it all figured out? It sounded that way. We need to know who you are and why you're here."

I must have read his scribbled critique a hundred times the next week. No way could I incorporate all of his advice into my next message. I felt he was holding me to an impossibly high standard. His approach was harsh and condemning, and I couldn't figure out his motive. But he was right on every point.

I went back the next week with a couple of improvements, and he met me at the door afterward with a qualified, "That was a *little* better. Now work on . . ."

For the next eighteen months, his less-than-tender critiques became not only the means by which my preaching improved but a means of grace—an inoculation against pride. After such an inauguration, I could not dare trust my sense of whether a sermon hit or missed. I preach knowing that, while few congregants listen with the sophisticated ear of my trainer, most are making judgments. I cannot preach only for the critics. I somehow must please an audience of One, while also being aware of the needs of many.

False motivators

While I've discovered I can't generate enough pride from preaching to keep me going, what else motivates me? The need to manipulate people? Maybe. Once I quit trying to be Mr. Intellectual and started telling smelly dog stories, I found that most people actually listened to me pretty well. Getting people to laugh can feel pretty good, and, in fact, can be intoxicating.

The pulpit gives one enormous leverage. Not only do I get to talk without being interrupted, but anything a pastor says from the pulpit takes on added significance. Even the announcements have added *gravitas* when promoted from the pulpit. Every leader of a floundering program tries to corner you before the service, vying for a public-service announcement of their ministry: "Don't forget to mention the men's prayer breakfast, pastor. Attendance has been poor lately."

What pastor on the planet hasn't, at least once,

used every bit of leverage at his disposal to staff the volunteer nursery? It's heady to feel people respond when you want them to, the way you want them to. But for me, the satisfaction of filling a slot is quickly pierced by my conscience reminding me that the pulpit is holy ground and using it to manipulate is unholy. I promise to stop (right after the nursery gets staffed). The wrong motive of manipulation, while always a temptation, can't sustain my passion to preach.

While searching for the source of my compulsion to preach, I thought about my need to be liked. We moved a lot in my early childhood, and as the skinny, new kid with big ears, I learned early that making people like me and making people laugh were effective ways to keep from getting beat up. It was easy to apply those principles to the sermon—*What these folks need is a message of encouragement.* Encouragement is one of my dominant spiritual gifts, so, when it comes to messages that cheer people up, I can deliver the mail.

But, after a while, the Jesus I preach begins to sound like the keynote speaker at a multilevel marketing convention. Preaching the whole counsel of God means occasionally putting on the mantle of the prophets and saying unequivocally, "Thus saith the Lord." It means overturning a few tables and, at times, taking up a whip in the temple.

That's not easy for me. People don't like prophets or people who meddle with profits. My hesitation is reinforced by my denomination, which sometimes defines "good preaching" as a spectacular delivery of verbal napalm. I don't want to perpetuate that. My goal in confrontive preaching is not simply to scorch a few eyebrows but to be a faithful proclaimer. On numerous occasions the biblical text and the Holy Spirit have forced me to say, loud and clear, "This is wrong. The Lord is not pleased."

But no matter how a preacher tries to couch tough truth in love, calling people to confession and repentance is a lonely job. When even your best friends shake your hand after worship without making eye contact, you realize that needing to be liked is a significant occupational hazard that must be overcome by anyone who desires to preach in a way that leads to the revival and renewal of the bride of Christ.

I realized that while needing to be liked was another temptation of mine, that couldn't fully explain my inner drive to preach the gospel.

My search for the wellspring of my compulsion took me back to the seventh grade. A college-age revivalist temporarily convinced our youth group that a life apart from full-time Christian service was a life wasted. He called for a public commitment of every youth present to go into the ministry. I was one of the last holdouts, but eventually even I followed the others like a lemming. I took his hand at the altar and mumbled something about "giving my life to God to use any way he wants to."

I figured out the next day that I'd been manipulated. No way would God hold me accountable for such a decision, but I wasn't sure if others would. Our church had no protocol for revoking a public decision, so I decided not to tell anyone about my second thoughts. Fortunately, no one seemed to take such decisions seriously, and I never heard another word about it.

Yet for years, even as a wayward young adult, in the night I would sometimes think of that decision and pray, "You know I didn't mean it then, but I'll still keep that promise if you can really use me."

Sixteen years after that junior high altar call, I quit my sales job to enroll in seminary. "Why are you doing this?" was the question asked by a concerned few. I couldn't adequately explain why then, or now. Certainly my reason was not out of a sense of obligation; it was a joyful response. In the movie *Chariots of Fire*, Eric Liddell tried to explain to his sister why he chose to prepare for the Olympic games rather than immediately return to China as a missionary: "When I run, I feel his pleasure."

That's the explanation of one who is called. God's call was a gracious invitation, not an order to be carried out. But I had the hardest time telling anyone that I was *called*.

That sounds, on the one hand, so presumptuous. It implies that out of all the people in this congregation, "God has set *me* apart to stand in this pulpit to speak for him, so listen up." And it feels so arcane. *Vocare*, the root word for "vocation," once meant a calling. Today it simply means "job." To be *called* to practice medicine, law, teaching, or preaching seems, at best, a noble notion from another century. Most people choose careers based on giftedness, interest, circumstance, and the likelihood that their choice will bring a significant financial return.

In a recent sermon featured on *Preaching Today*, William Willimon pointed out that all believers are called—called to be disciples. He's right, of course. My calling is, in one sense, no different from any other believer. I've discovered my spiritual gifts and seek to use them where they produce the greatest fruit. For me, for now, that means preaching and writing.

But I sense there is something more. My pulse quickens when I read Paul's instructions for Timothy: "Preach the Word; be prepared in season and out of season; correct, rebuke and encourage—with great patience and careful instruction" (2 Tim. 4:2, NIV). That's the headwaters of a wide stream feeding my passion for preaching. I'm as compelled to preach as that smelly old dog was compelled to track. Neither can be judged by appearance. I know my Master's pleasure when I preach. My motives are not always pure, but they are, somehow, pure enough for God to use to bring fruit. And that's all the motive I need to keep preaching with passion.

9

BUT DO YOU LOVE ME?

I WAS WORKING on an issue of *Preaching Today* when the phone rang. "Pastor Ed?" asked the uncertain woman on the other end. I didn't recognize the voice. My mental Rolodex started spinning.

"This is Jean McGuire."

My mind was still blank. "From Arizona," she continued.

My mind stopped spinning just in time: Jean was a faithful attendee of our last church but so shy and reclusive that I never got more than a whispered hello and a downward glance when I greeted her on Sunday mornings. What could have motivated this timid creature to make a long-distance call to a former pastor she hadn't seen in more than two years?

"Well, hello, Jean. What a surprise! It's good to hear from you."

Embarrassed silence.

"I'm sorry to bother you. Maybe I shouldn't have called, but . . . well, I'm calling about Roy."

Roy was her forty-something, never married son. He was a huge man, intimidating in both size and stoicism.

"How's my old buddy Roy doing?"

She blurted, "He died last month."

"What? He died? Roy? What happened?"

She went on to explain a lengthy hospital stay for phlebitis, complicated by obesity, poor circulation, and high blood pressure. While she spoke, my thoughts were churning: They had no friends that I knew of. Did anyone else in the church even know of her loss? I hoped their new pastor knew and ministered to their family.

"I'm so sorry, Jean. If I had known Roy was in the hospital, I'd have called him and prayed with him."

"I know, Pastor Ed. He really wanted to talk with you, too, but I could never find your new address or phone number. But today I was cleaning out his room and I found it. I knew you'd want to hear about it. You know that Roy always said you was the best friend he ever had."

The second punch hit me harder than the first. *Best friend?* I hardly knew the man. We'd had a couple of brief counseling sessions when he was facing some difficulties in his job, and I invited him to lunch a time or two after that.

"Roy meant a lot to me as well." (That is, what little of Roy I came to know. I didn't lie.)

"We could tell. No pastor ever took much notice of us before you came. Roy always came home from church sayin', 'That preacher's been readin' my mail again.' He'd sit on the couch after dinner and read his notes from your sermon and just shake his head and ask, 'How'd he know, Momma? How'd he know?'"

We spoke a while longer. I prayed with her, then hung up the phone, shut my office door, and broke down. I grieved Roy's death and his mother's loss, but mostly I grieved the loneliness of a person whose best friend was the preacher who usually spoke to him over a microphone from forty feet away.

That phone call put me in a tailspin for days. I should have felt grateful that Roy called me "friend," but inside an accusing voice whispered, *Too little, too late,* tempting me to believe I had neglected him. Should I have pushed past his intimidating exterior?

For a few days, Roy came to represent every church member I'd ever failed to care for in a crisis. I replayed every brief encounter with him I could recall, searching for clues about why he came to view me as his best friend. There wasn't much to recall. I'd ask about his mom, his job, and his old dog, then he'd bring up church. I remembered he always commented about my sermons, the kind preachers like to hear: "You really got me to thinking about . . ."

I never put much stock in such appraisals. I figured he was just being polite, trying to make small talk about our one and only point of connection. Roy would usually allude to something going on in his interior life but in cryptic fashion, as if I already knew the details.

"You made me think about . . . well, you know, that thing I was depressed about."

"Tell me about it."

147

Roy would laugh. "Oh, you know, Pastor. You preached about it the last two Sundays." It never went any further than that.

I don't remember ever hearing Roy specifically articulate the nature of his spiritual struggles, but his allusions and my intuition told me that they probably had to do with his worth in the eyes of God. It was a major theme of my preaching during that time, and I always tried to affirm him, assuring him that he really was a beloved child of God.

But I never saw more than glimmers of belief, and I had a church full of people to minister to, sermons to preach, programs to administrate. As big as Roy was, he was easy to lose in the shuffle.

My last Sunday at that church, Roy grabbed me in a wordless, sweaty, vertebrae-snapping hug before charging out the door to his truck. For me it was just one of many hugs from parishioners we had come to love. But Roy, I know now, was saying good-bye to his very best friend.

Can a sermon, a monologue, really touch lives in such a relational way?

Though gratified to know I made a small difference in Roy's life, I've wondered lately about how other parishioners perceive their relationship with the one who proclaims God's Word for them Sunday after Sunday. While many, maybe most, would not consider the preacher their best friend, I suspect quite a few would form their understanding of that relationship based on how they receive that preacher's preaching.

Jean's phone call helped me realize how much pastoral care happens during a sermon. It certainly wasn't eloquence or persuasiveness or great logic that made Roy feel my friendship. I think it had everything to do with him sensing, mostly through my preaching, that I loved him and knew he was listening.

Loving the jerks

In a lecture at Beeson Divinity School, Dr. Elizabeth Achtemeier told of a former student who couldn't preach. She struggled to understand what was wrong, until he started talking about his congregation: "They're all a bunch of stupid jerks," he said. Achtemeier stated unequivocally, "It is impossible to preach to people you hate."

While that may seem obvious, her point underscores the fact that effective preaching is at least one part relationship. How does a pastor preach so the people feel loved?

I certainly never felt loved by most of the preachers of my childhood. I remember Brother Bob—loud, emotional, animated—but we left each Sunday with the weight of our sin increased; our sense of unworthiness magnified. Hope was never proffered to our souls.

Our next preacher was so emotionally unstable he cried during most every sermon. Passionate? Nah, just really, really sad. Then there was the youth revivalist who could have made better money as a stand-up comic; he was that funny, but no one would have described him as passionate. Along the way there were also those who seemed as if they were above touching the heart; they seemed to think of themselves as the learned, the sophisticated, the cerebral. What they said may have been theologically accurate but was neutered, cut off, and separate from the world of sadness and anger and insecurity that we inhabited.

Many preachers argue that such emotion, or lack thereof, is a result of passion—for God and his Word, for study, for truth. But preaching is more than a passionate delivery or funny story or a biblical teaching. Preaching is touching, and spiritually passionate preaching is rooted not only in loving God but in loving people. Words, no matter how eloquent, profound, or funny, may not communicate the clearest message. My delivery of touch tells people everything about how I really feel about them. A gentle hand on the shoulder is one kind of touch. A warm hug is another. A slap, a shake, or a stiff finger in the sternum are others.

Preaching provides me with the opportunity to touch more people in thirty minutes than I could possibly minister to in a week of conventional pastoral care. If people have found in me a high level of trust and respect for God and his Word, if they sense in me an authentic spirit, if they hear from me messages of encouragement, trust, and hope, then the Holy Spirit finds hearts and wills open to transformation by the gospel.

In this together

In my early attempts to communicate "I am one of you"—and thus build a relationship with my congregations—my basic approach was to preface every point with "I struggle with this too." I never gave examples, or if I did, they were trite and sterile.

But in a sermon about loneliness, just before Easter one year, I stumbled upon a more effective way of opening myself up to the congregation—and thus connecting with them on a heart level. My text was from Matthew 26: Jesus, the night of his arrest, saw his closest friends desert him.

"What does it feel like to be abandoned and left all alone?" I asked. I then told of the loneliest period of my life, in the months and years following a broken engagement with a girl I had dated throughout high school. Afterward, I was overwhelmed with the people who wanted to talk with me about lost loves—tales of divorces, infidelities, engagements, and near engagements. Everyone, it seemed, had been hurt by a love that had grown cold and died. In telling about my loneliness, we all went home a little less lonely that day.

However, as much as I want to connect with my listeners, no one really wants to hear the details about my current inner battles with doubt, pride, dissatisfaction, anger, lust, or ambition. No one really wants to see me emotionally disrobe in the pulpit. Perhaps it's enough to allude to current battles. But that can never include even the sketchiest details about sexual temptation. And stories about current financial struggles are tricky; they can too easily be interpreted as dissatisfaction with my salary or the church.

I've concluded that if I'm going to connect with people in the pulpit, perhaps the best way is to tell stories of victory over temptations in the past. If I've found God sufficient in moments of pain or loss or insecurity, if I'm safely past the point where people might wonder about my spiritual or emotional stability, then I try to pass on that wisdom to my listeners.

I don't care about being vulnerable—a popular word among preachers trying to be relevant these days. My motive is not to be perceived as real or authentic. The cliché "Sharing the gospel is just one beggar telling another beggar where he found bread" is still one of the best descriptions of the preacher's task.

You can do this

I was fortunate to live in the Chicago area during the basketball dynasty of the Chicago Bulls, led by Michael Jordan. Watching Jordan play basketball was one of life's great pleasures. Not only does he perform midair magic with a basketball, he appears to have both a winsome personality and dynamic leadership ability. While we admire such persons, we are intimidated by them at the same time. I have marveled at Jordan countless times, but only in my wildest dreams have I said to myself, *I bet I could do that.*

Brian Williams, on the other hand, made me think a career in the NBA was still a possibility for me. Acquired by the Bulls late in the 1996–1997 season, Williams was overweight and a bit slow. As the season progressed into the playoffs, he not only made some memorable plays but a number of spectacular bloopers as well. But overall, his stats proved him more asset than liability. Williams was the Simon Peter of the Bulls, a person we could relate to because he is more like you and me.

In my work at LEADERSHIP, I met some nationally known pastors who are the Michael Jordans of the preaching vocation—unusually good-looking, incredibly smart, influential, and driven by the passion of their calling. They inspire me in one sense, yet often after hearing them speak, I've come away feeling more intimidated than helped. I look at what they've accomplished and know I will never have that level of impact.

Yet there have been others who have made an impact on me precisely because when I watch them preach and lead, I feel, *I can do this.* Maybe that was part of the reason Roy felt we were friends. Maybe he figured, *If Ed can make it, so can I.* I never want to preach in such a way that portrays my life as being so far above the crowd that others stand in awe, certain they can never achieve the spiritual heights that I describe. Spiritually passionate preaching never elevates the preacher above the listener.

I know you're here

A young woman left my office smiling one day. She had just unburdened herself by telling me her secret of bulimia, which had kept her down for more than a decade. She said my seven-week series of messages on our freedom in Christ gave her the courage to tell me about it. Over the course of the series, I had tried to raise every issue I could think of that might keep someone in bondage to their past. During one message from Romans 8:1–2 on "Our Freedom From Condemnation," I said, "Maybe you were abused as a child, and made to feel it was your fault. Maybe you were told you were stupid, and were constantly criticized by your parents. . . . There is hope for you in Christ. There is freedom from condemnation."

That young woman confided in me that she became bulimic, in part, because of her inability to live up to the standards of perfectionistic parents. That one line in a sermon had caught her by surprise. "How did you know I needed to hear those very words?" she asked.

"I guess the Holy Spirit knew you needed to hear them, so he gave them to me to say," I replied for the second time that day.

Just a few hours earlier, I had met with a man who, also for the first time, told me his shameful secret of being molested as a little boy. "I never heard anyone bring that up in a sermon before," he told me. "I figured that I must be the only damaged goods in this congregation. But when I heard you say it right out loud like that, I figured it must affect a lot of people or you wouldn't have bothered to mention it. So I figured maybe we could talk about it without your being disgusted with me."

While a seminary student learns in his first pastorate that a person's appearance offers little or no clues to a person's soul, I'm still amazed at how outward appearances can deceive. I've ministered in an affluent, well-put-together suburb, a transitioning urban area of dwindling hope, and a small-town, rural church where poverty hung like dust. In all three places, I've encountered similar pain, confusion, bondage, and fear. In any setting, preaching must free people from the pain of the past, communicating, "I know you're here, I'm not surprised by your past, and this is for you, too."

Collateral benefits

When I approach the pulpit with the intent of administering spiritual care to people I love, when I'm appropriately honest about my spiritual ups and downs, when I demonstrate that the Christian life is attainable and doable, when I communicate, *I know you're here,* some tremendous benefits emerge:

1. *I lower my counseling load.* Several examples in this chapter came from conversations in my counseling office, which is where I've heard people clearly articulate the results of preaching as pastoral care. And many of those who came for pastoral care had pinpointed the issue in their lives as a result of the message; I didn't have to fish for their spiritual illness, and that saved us many hours. But many more, I believe, never felt the need to come see me because the Bible's truth, clearly articulated and applied, did its transforming work without a trip to my office. That is one more reason why I'm passionate about preaching.

I then get to relate to these people, not as the wise, omnipotent counselor, but as the friend who was able to give them the key piece of information needed to unlock their own dilemmas. In such situations, I'm only the messenger, and they are much more likely to thank God than to thank me for the change that comes.

2. *I can better preach the severe passages.* Pastoral preaching allows me to preach prophetically without rancor. Not that I haven't preached harsh messages in anger; in previous chapters I told about my shortcomings in that area.

I was recently talking about this with Johnny Hunt, a pastor from Georgia. "It's the most amazing thing," he said. "When people know you love them, you can shoot straight from the hip about the seven churches of Revelation, and people will come up after the message and say, 'That really encouraged me.' If they had heard my words without the filter of love, they could only have been offended!"

3. *They think I'm a better preacher than I am.* It happened frequently enough to be predictable. Someone would send me a sermon tape of their pastor, wanting me to consider it for *Preaching Today.* The letter often read something like, "Our pastor is one of the greatest preachers you will ever hear. He preached this message I'm sending you just a month after he got us through my mother's funeral. . . . I know it will touch you and your listeners as much as it touched me."

It may have been a good sermon, but it usually never made the final cut for *Preaching Today.* Because she felt loved by her pastor, to her, his sermons were world class. I'm always delighted when someone believes her preacher is one of the best communicators alive.

I don't know about you, but I can live with people thinking I'm a better preacher than I really am.

10

FREED FROM CONTROL

FROM MY THIRD GRADE year through junior high, our family moved frequently. Being the new kid can be tough enough, but I was somewhat small for my age and had begun to wear glasses, and that made me an easy target for playground bullies and their hangers-on. I tried to deal with conflict by learning how to fight, but soon discovered I was much better at talking my way out of a mess than fighting my way out. In fact, one bully became one of my closest friends. Of course, by then I had "hit my growth"; perhaps that helped, too.

That early training in persuasive speaking served me well in life. As a hunting guide, I convinced men more than twice my age that I was indeed skilled and dependable enough for them to entrust with their lives for a week in the wilderness. During a four-year stint in the U.S. Air Force, I supervised skilled people, many of them older than me, when most others my age were still attending frat parties.

Based on my prior experience and giftedness, when I finally got around to attending college, I chose a major in communications. Particularly satisfying were my classes in persuasion, learning how to move people toward a decision. I became a sales representative in the financial services business; I seemed to have a knack for closing the deal.

I learned how to make the most of my persuasive gifts. So when I made the decision to enter pastoral ministry, I believed my abilities to make things happen and to influence people would be a great asset—for the kingdom, of course. And surely that would be most evident in the pulpit.

This was all long before I began to pay attention to the character of an Old Testament persuader who had also learned to make his living by his wits. Jacob, son of Isaac, would have been the superstar of any used-car sales force. He had a sharp mind, a silver tongue, and absolutely no scruples.

When we eavesdrop on Jacob in Genesis 27, we hear him telling his mother, in King James language, "Behold, Esau my brother is a hairy man, and I am a *smooth* man." His literal meaning was, "I can't grow a whisker, while my brother is the human sweater."

But I can't read this passage without thinking how much it serves as a description of his character as defined by his name: "He grasps the heel," was sort of like, "He pulls your leg." It could be translated "deceiver" or "smooth operator." Jacob was a natural born con artist; he had a smooth way of always getting just what he wanted. The context of this self-revelatory statement, "I am a smooth man," is just prior to the con he pulled on his blind, feeble old daddy, Isaac.

Almost toothless, the creaky patriarch had a hankering for one last meal of tender young venison, so he sent his favorite boy Esau out to the woods. "Prepare it just the way I like it so it's savory and good, and bring it here for me to eat. Then I will pronounce the blessing that belongs to you, my firstborn son, before I die" (Gen. 27:4, NLT).

Smooth-talking, smooth-walking Jacob, ever the manipulator, ever the control freak, wanted one more thing from his older-by-just-a-minute brother. He'd already snatched the elder son's share of the inheritance from Esau in exchange for a bowl of stew. (The big, hairy redneck had no grasp of the concept of delayed gratification.) Here was opportunity knocking at Jacob's door.

Their mother, Rebekah, had the makings of a grifter herself. She sent her "mama's boy" out to the herd to butcher a couple of kid goats.

After preparing the meal, Rebekah secured the goat skins to Jacob's smooth arms and neck. He put on the hairy brother's clothes, probably rolled in the compost pile to approximate Esau's earthy smell, then approached the bed of the old man with a tray holding savory meat and hot biscuits on one of Rebekah's good plates.

Even in his aged state, Isaac was not senile. His sight might have been gone, but his ears still worked—and that tenor voice sounded like Jacob, not his wild man Esau. His hands could still feel, and did. Sure enough, this man bearing supper had arms as hairy as a goat's backside. Ah, but did he smell like the wilderness? That was the true test. At Isaac's request, Mr. Smooth leaned over his daddy and gave him a noseful. His trickery succeeded. Convinced at last that he was really dealing with Esau, Isaac gave his patriarchal blessing to the wrong son.

Jacob was used to getting his way. And once again he proved he knew just how to control the people and situations in his life so as to achieve the desired outcome. Later he would meet his match in his future father-in-law, Laban, but for the most part, Jacob got whatever Jacob desired.

Control freaks anonymous

None of us would be thrilled to discover that a small but malignant portion of our drive to preach well, to preach with passion, comes from a desire to control people. I can think of no deeper disappointment with myself than this self-revelation. Hiding beneath my sincere desire to see people grow in their faith, to see our church grow in effectiveness, was an insecure little boy who wanted to make sure that no one outsmarted him, that things unfolded according to his plan, that no one ever took advantage of him again.

I realize now that, in my application of all I had read and learned about preaching, I was hoping, in part, to discover the keys to the flip side of persuasion; that is, manipulation. My goals, I would have insisted, were benevolent, not evil like some people's, of course. Therefore, they justified a little arm twisting now and then.

Like the evangelists of my childhood, I wanted to be able to turn up the volume and the heat, until every sinner within earshot fell to his or her knees and cried out for mercy. We Baptists are big on "walking the aisle." While the congregation sings a hymn of commitment, the preacher exhorts people to come pray to receive Christ or kneel at the altar as a public acknowledgment that the sermon touched them.

I can't recall too many altar calls I've given to which someone didn't respond. Maybe it was a cartoon I saw, or maybe too many episodes of "Hogan's Heroes," but I can see myself as the commandant, dressed in black leather, slapping my palm with a whip and saying in a bad German accent, "Ve haf vays of making you valk."

Okay, that's a bit overstated, but surely calling someone to repentance is an acceptable use of manipulation, er, I mean, persuasion. And who could object if I were successful at encouraging people to read their Bibles more? And what if I could talk people into praying more? Nothing wrong with that, is there? Most days, I'd resort to just about any measure, without a trace of guilt, if I could figure out a way to get people just to *be nice* to one another.

Jacob's name was a play on Hebrew words that

sounded like heel-grabber. Preachers like me often yearn to be the heart-grabber, the conscience-grabber, and, sometimes, the throat-grabber. In my zeal, I can mistake badgering, bullying, browbeating, coercing, wheedling, and nagging for passionate preaching. A man in a former congregation once told me, "I don't feel like I've been to preachin' if my ribs ain't bruised when I leave."

Why should anyone be surprised when one of us, schooled in this type of preaching, gets our own television show and, before we know it, starts hoodwinking little old ladies out of their social security checks in order to pay for the airtime? Believe me, that's not a long step from shaming someone into signing up to be a nursery worker.

Don't breathe easy if you don't fit the stereotype. Just because we fail to shout, stomp, snort, and spit when we preach, just because we don't hawk our merchandise over a toll-free number doesn't exonerate us from the charge of manipulative preaching.

Some preachers are blessed (or cursed) with a measure of *duende*, the power to attract and influence through a charming personality. Winsomeness can be a dangerous thing. While screening tapes for *Preaching Today* (and even my own), I heard a style of manipulative preaching that is beyond the caricature. Usually it's from sophisticated, well-educated preachers with voices like honey butter. The finely tuned insinuation, just the right touch of well-placed guilt, the understated application of shame, all of these can go a long way toward controlling the immediate actions, if not the long-term behavior, of congregants.

Measuring our control

In the months I worked on this book, I scratched out a dozen different chapter outlines on how to measure the results of a sermon. It's something most preachers want to know. *How'd I do?* we start wondering immediately after the benediction. As we shake hands with congregants, our minds are keeping score. There's the predictable "Nice job" or "Good sermon, Pastor" (worth just a point), the nice-to-hear "Boy, you've been reading my mail" (5 points), to the highly prized "That message really touched me. Could we talk about some things later this week?" (a whopping 25 points).

The attempt to measure effectiveness continues after I get home. At the dinner table, I hound my wife, Susan, "So, what did you think?"

"About what?" she invariably asks.

"The sermon. How'd it go?"

"Oh. It was fine." (Subtract 5 points.)

"I had trouble following you this morning for some reason." (Subtract 20 points.)

"Where did you get that story you told about our vacation? I don't remember anything like that ever happening." (Subtract 50 points.)

Earlier, I discussed the tendency to overestimate the effectiveness of a single sermon and underestimate the net result over time for someone who digests our preaching on a regular basis. Any attempt to measure effectiveness is guesswork at best, so I scrapped my attempts to quantify results for any one message. More importantly, I came to realize that, for me, attempting to control the outcome in order to more accurately measure my effectiveness could easily degenerate into just another expression of this desire to control people.

I never used to think of myself as a controlling person, until I was waylaid recently by a passionate sermon entitled "The Breaking of a Control Freak," based on the further exploits of our man Jacob, Mr. Smooth.

After several Sundays away preaching, I attended our home church with my family. Our pastor took Genesis 32 as his text. Now, Rob, at least in his preaching, seems to be the antithesis of a control freak. As a leader, he's a great consensus builder. As a preacher, his approach is usually quite understated, more didactic than pragmatic. He'll say stuff like "May I suggest to you . . ." I can't imagine anyone ever feeling manipulated by his sermons. Nonetheless, not long ago, he hit me between the eyes.

He set the stage by telling us, from verses 7 and 8, that control freaks usually operate out of insecurity and fear. Boy, he was right on that count. I was taking notes but thinking about all the people I've known who fit that category. People I've worked for. People who have worked for me. My drill sergeant. Denom-

inational types. Other pastors who run their congregations with an iron fist. *Yeah, these people really have
a problem. I hope he can get the attention of any control
freaks we have in this congregation.* I looked around the
crowd with interest, trying to guess who was going to
be nailed by this message, hoping everyone who
needed it was listening.

Rob went on to verses 13–15. Jacob hopes to buy
off Esau's anger with a substantial bribe. He took that
opportunity to define a control freak as "one who
does inappropriate things to manage the outcome of
a situation." Busted. Had Rob looked my way, he
would have noticed my deer-in-the-headlights look.

I quit glancing around and began to pay attention
to my own heart, especially when the preacher got to
verses 22 and following. I needed to hear a word of
hope for *me* as he described how God broke the cycle
of control and manipulation in Jacob that night be-
side the Jabbok river.

Wrestling with God

As cryptic as the identity of the wrestler in the
other corner of the ring is in that passage, something
profound happened to Jacob that night. The masked
man (who was really an angel, or God, or the prein-
carnate Christ, depending on your commentary) put
a move on the Tenacious Trickster that made his sci-
atic nerve begin to scream with pain. Even then Jacob
would not give up without getting something out of

the encounter. "I'll let go when you bless me," he said with a grimace.

Jacob became "Israel" that day, because "you have struggled with God and with men and have overcome." Jacob the *trickster* became Israel the *prevailer*. The conniver came face-to-face with the Covenanter. Jacob had a new name and a limp to remind him forever of that long night at Peniel.

That Sunday morning, I had a series of flashbacks to my own wrestling matches with God:

Flashback 1: Remember that first church plant I told you about? My role was to be a catalyst; once the new work was firmly on its feet, I would move on, presumably to begin another new work. (It was a strategy widely practiced in my denomination in those days that, thankfully, is now regarded as flawed.)

That work grew quickly. I grew quickly—especially in my preaching. I would never have pleaded guilty to the charge that I preached to tickle itching ears, but I was definitely too close to the line for safety. After the encounter with the professional communicator, that ego-busting experience I wrote about in an earlier chapter, I soon learned some tricks of the trade. If attention seemed to be wandering, I employed certain phrases that immediately elicited a nonvocal response from most and a hearty amen from a few transplanted Texans in the crowd. I was able to use humor effectively, so I spent a significant amount of prep time each week figuring out how to solicit laughter.

Always the pragmatist, I liked results. And we seemed to be getting them. I couldn't buy enough church-growth material: it promised results, and I loved the feeling of controlling our destiny. It looked like I was well on my way toward becoming the successful pastor and preacher I had set out to become.

Flashback 2: After graduating early from seminary, I sat home taking care of our first daughter for six months while waiting for a place to serve. We finally hooked up with a church in the Southwest that had virtually died but wanted to begin all over again. Unable to discern the differences in skills needed to deliver a new birth, which I had used in the church plant, and the skills needed to resuscitate the terminally ill, which I had never attempted to use, I accepted the challenge. After all, I was pretty persuasive, pretty smooth. If anyone could make it happen, I reasoned, I could. I went for it.

The denomination promised us financial support for just a short period; the denominational types wanted results as much as I did. So I went after them with a passion. I preached hard. I twisted arms. I drove people. I used people.

You *must* come to faith in Christ. You've got to *work harder*, make more sacrifices. It's absolutely *imperative* our offerings increase by 35 percent this year, or we're doomed.

Sixteen months later, the whole thing folded. I had failed. I left that ministry limping, forever crippled. (In my mind, "crippled" was pretty much the same as "rendered useless.")

A few months before we left, a neighboring church burned and needed to borrow our folding chairs for the facility they were renting in the interim. We had plenty to spare, so we loaded them in a pickup one hot August night, just about dusk. As the locusts began to buzz, the pastor and I stood around talking. He looked at our pathetic building and said, "Ed, I don't know what God wants to do here with this church, but I'm convinced he wants to make a humble man out of you."

Flashback 3: After finding initial success in my writing, when the opportunity came to join the staff of LEADERSHIP, I struggled with doubt. *Can I really do this? What if I fail?* These questions had never been uttered by my lips before. Nonetheless, I knew unmistakably that God was leading, and the thought became *I must do this.*

Something had changed within me. Somewhere between success and failure, something new within me was born. Instead of asking, *Can I control the situation? Can I manage the processes and outcomes? Will I be successful at this?* I narrowed my questions to one: *Is God leading? If so, I will follow without regard to outcome.*

Those three snapshots of character-shaping events took place in a matter of seconds. As a recipient of the sermon, I felt the supernatural effect of the Word that morning. Jacob's story became my story. I was the man who had wrestled with God at Peniel and walked away richer for having been crippled by him.

I was both convicted of my ongoing tendencies to control in other areas of life and strangely warmed to discover that, at least in some areas of my life, God was breaking the control that controlling has on the controller.

Until that sermon, I had not completely grasped all that God had accomplished in me through my greatest success and my greatest failure in ministry. That initial success had reinforced my belief that I could make things happen. My subsequent failure was the beginning (and it's a work still in progress) of the end of trying to control the outcome of ministry, including the outcome of the sermon.

Which was better? Success or failure? The surprising answer is "failure." I know now that I can't change anyone. Not my wife or my daughters, my colleagues, and especially those to whom I preach. I've had to come to terms with the fact that I can't assess changes in them with any more accuracy than I can assess changes in myself.

Who's responsible?

So if manipulative preaching and trying to control the results is the behavior of a control freak, is that a case for bland preaching that never calls for a response from people?

Obviously not. Jesus, as revealed in the Gospels, was full of *duende*. Compassionate, charming, and yes, persuasive. He wasn't afraid to challenge the disciples to lay down their nets and ledger books to become disciples. He got results but he didn't seek results. He sought relationships. He sought reconciliation, man with God. He sought restoration of lost sheep to their Shepherd.

I am not God. I am not Jesus Christ. And I am not the Holy Spirit. Being able to say, mean, and understand the implications of these three statements can be the first step toward liberation for a control freak. It means that none of their jobs are vacant, nor will they ever be, nor will I ever possess the skills to do their jobs. Therefore, the best I can do is believe Jesus' words, "Remain in me, and I will remain in you. No branch can bear fruit by itself; it must remain in the vine. Neither can *you* bear fruit unless you remain in me" (John 15:4, NIV, emphasis mine).

So what's the antidote for control freaks? According to the sermon I heard from Rob Bugh, it comes when we firmly grasp the reality and the consequences of this truth—God is calling the shots, not me. He alone can accurately assess the outcome. Therefore, I will not ask, "Will this message be well-received, connecting people at their point of felt needs?" I will ask, "Is God leading me to preach this text?" The first question gives the preacher a passion of sorts, anticipating the end result. The second, however, empowers us to stand and deliver both healing and severe words with equal fervor. Preachers never again need to be apologetic for preaching about stewardship, repentance, or commitment, if the right question is asked, which the preacher will never ask if he needs to maintain control over the outcome.

The crippled Jacob/Israel could never have predicted, controlled, or manipulated the circumstances of the following day. As he limped toward his big, red, hairy brother, he was totally unprepared to meet a man whose heart had been changed—not by bribery, but by God. Instead of hatred and a sharp spear, he was greeted with a sweaty hug, a kiss, and tears of joy.

What's going to happen next Sunday when I preach? I don't know and I won't hazard a guess. Some may hug me, others may curse me. Some will think I'm profound, others will think I'm shallow.

I cannot control any response but my own. And here's my best response: Study hard. Be creative. Challenge people. Use *duende*, but don't rely on it. Crucify my will. Draw passion from obedience, and leave the results to God.

Preaching is a lot more freeing that way. And passion flows from the heart set free from the need to control.